LOVE
our City

HOW WE LOVE OUR NEIGHBOR AS WE LOVE OURSELVES

TOMMY *"URBAN D."* KYLLONEN

Tranzlation Leadership

TAMPA, FL

Tranzlation Leadership™
1235 E. Fowler Ave. Tampa, FL 33612
© 2026 Tommy Kyllonen

While all stories in this book are true, some names and identifying information may have been changed to protect the privacy of individuals.

Cover + Interior Design: Josué Marrero / Dreamery Collective™
www.dreamerycollective.com

Photography: Crossover Church Social Media Team

ISBN: 979-8-218-91806-4

This book is also available in ebook and audio formats

Printed in the United States of America

www.loveourcitybook.com
www.tranzlationleadership.com

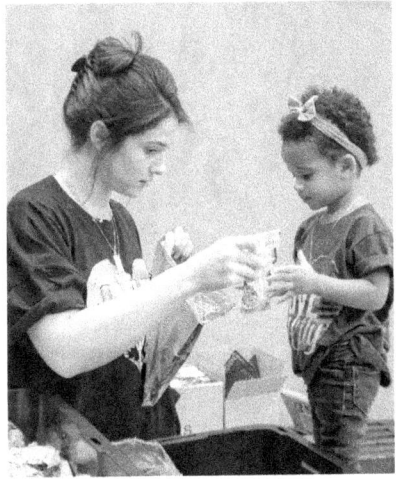

*TABLE OF CONTENTS

INTRODUCTION

I thought I was just going to play basketball. But what happened on that court in the summer of 1993 changed someone's eternity and helped shape the direction of my ministry. I was home on summer break from college, where I was studying to be in youth ministry. As I was shooting around, I connected with this guy named Carlos. We talked about basketball and Hip-Hop. As we got comfortable with each other, we weaved God into the conversation. I told him I was going to school in Florida and that I was studying to work with youth through a church. Carlos was curious about Florida, and I wanted to dedicate my life to working with youth in a church.

He shared with me that he had never attended a Christian church in his life. His family was Catholic, but only by title. He had only attended a Catholic church a few times when he was a kid. Wow… a guy who never went to church. I heard about people like him, but I rarely met one. So I invited him to come to the church I was attending. He said yes! I was excited. That Sunday, I had a seat saved for him, and I told a few people that my new friend Carlos was coming to church. I kept looking back and looking back, but Carlos never showed.

The next week, I ran into him again at the basketball courts and asked him what happened on Sunday, and he told me that he forgot and that he would come this Sunday. You can guess what happened that Sunday. No show.

The following week, when I saw him on the courts, I got his phone number, and I told him I would come and pick him up for church. He only lived 3 blocks away from the church, but I offered him a ride to make sure he would really come this time. That Sunday, Carlos came to church, and it was a day I'll never forget. I realized how weird Christians are. I grew up in church, so I was used to most of the traditions, even if they weren't my style. But Carlos had never set foot in that type of environment. So that day, I put myself in his shoes and tried to experience it through his eyes. It was painful.

First off, I realized our hospitality was lacking, as he wasn't welcomed by anyone. Secondly, I noticed that he was dressed in jeans and a T-Shirt and everyone else was dressed up. I thought it wouldn't be a big deal, but it seemed to be as others were staring. This immediately made him feel awkward. On top of that, he was the only Hispanic in the room. I knew the diversity of the church was almost non-existent, but I was hopeful he would be embraced. Not really the result. Then came all of the questions. What does that song mean? Why did they say that? He wasn't complaining. He just had honest questions. Some of them I could easily answer, and some of them had me thinking, "Why do we do that?" I felt like I was a translator because we were speaking a foreign language.

It was an epiphany moment that rocked me to the core. It began to shape my ministry philosophy for the future. I didn't have all the details mapped out, but I knew I wanted to create a church that would truly Love Our City and when they came to our house they would be welcomed. Guests would be able to connect with the music, the language and the dress code. They would be able to walk in and see someone that looked like them. This became super important to me. The church I was attending said they wanted to show the love of Christ to the community, but there wasn't anything tangible that they ever did. Carlos lived just three blocks away and nobody in the church looked like him, his family, or many of his neighbors. This forever changed my thinking about my church and my neighbors.

I'm grateful you picked up this book, and you are going on this journey with us to learn to better love our neighbors. At the end of each chapter, you will find some questions and some space for you to write down some personal application and some notes. There is also a video series that you can watch on YouTube each week (Click on the QR code at the end of each week) and take some notes here in the book as it ties in the themes from the week. Hopefully, you can watch this with a small group and participate in the discussion questions together. Before your reading is over, we're also encouraging you to engage in a Love Our City community service project. This will probably be something with your church or your small group. If they aren't hosting any projects, it is something you could create yourself with a group of friends, co-workers, or family.

So you might be wondering what happened to Carlos. He didn't come back to church right away, but I kept building with him, and he soon started a relationship with Christ. He has been through some ups and downs in the past couple of decades, but back in 2017, I flew back to Pennsylvania and was the best man in his wedding. He and his wife are serving Christ, involved in their local church, and God is doing some great things in his life that all sparked from that basketball court back in 1993. I'm praying that you'll have some basketball court encounters over the next few weeks that will change the course of your neighbor's eternity. I'm praying that God will awaken some new things inside of your heart that will change the way you look at your city. We have a team of people praying for you and your neighbors. Let's get ready to Love Our City!

THE STORY

y Love Our City story started more than thirty years ago. I was fresh out of Bible College and launched an urban youth ministry at a small church plant in Tampa, Florida. I am an artist and a creative, so I had lots of out-of-the-box ideas. Looking back at it now, I was way ahead of my time. I was criticized, questioned, hated, and told that what I was doing would never become self-sustainable. But I was passionate, entrepreneurial, and driven to see people come to know Jesus. Hip-Hop Music and Sports were my two biggest tools in my early years of ministry. Our church gained recognition for hosting basketball leagues, Hip-Hop concerts, and incorporating that culture into our weekly youth services. Within a few years, we grew to become the largest youth ministry in our city. The majority of our teens and young adults were unchurched. Their families didn't come to our small church on Sunday mornings. These teens were reached through our outreach efforts and began attending church on their own. Many of them were soon on fire for God and started witnessing to their parents and bringing them to church.

In 2002, I was pushed into becoming the Lead Pastor at the church. We only had forty adults, and 90% of them were under thirty years old, including my wife and me. We were short on resources, maturity, and people… but we had lots of freedom to reshape and recreate what church could look like in our context. A big focus was reaching unchurched and dechurched people in our community. We created a fresh expression of worship and teaching that started attracting lots of new people. It was a big deal back then for people not have to dress up to go to church. We created a casual, multi-ethnic, non-judgmental environment that most people had never experienced. I've always worn sneakers on Sundays, which eventually became more mainstream with pastors. That alone made so many people feel comfortable and connected. We continued to use music and sports as an outreach tool as we built basketball courts and a skate park on our church campus. We added some food programs and classes to help people with finances. Within a few years, our little church building was bursting at the seams on Sundays, and we had to add a second service and then a third. We even built an outdoor overflow room (you can do that in Florida). We loved our city, and more and more people were coming to experience the love of Jesus.

God gave us a vision to move to a bigger space to love even more of our city. It seemed like an impossible dream as we still didn't have the resources to go to that next level. The next few years, we focused on spiritual growth and maturity. In 2008, we felt the green light to move forward to go after that bigger space. We set our eyes on a former Toys' R' Us building on a main street in the heart of the city. It was seven times larger than our old facility. It was a pretty crazy dream. How could we ever afford to make a move like that? Especially when we started fundraising and trying to sell our old facility in the middle of the Great Recession. But those are the type of situations where you can't take any credit. It didn't make sense on paper, but God kept opening each door little by little over the next two years. In 2009, we did our first outreach in the abandoned Toys R' Us parking lot. We gave away 300 backpacks for children going back to school. We had a hip-hop concert, free food, and lots of love. Even though the building wasn't ours yet, we were claiming that ground, stepping out on faith, and demonstrating to God how we were going to use that property. In March of 2010, we signed the deal with Toys R' Us, and construction began to retrofit 43,000 square feet of empty space into a church. It was miracle after miracle that I share in detail in my "ReBuild" book.

Crossover Church miraculously hosted the ten-year anniversary of our Flavor Fest Leadership Conference and Music Festival the weekend of 10/10/10. A few weeks later, we had the grand opening for our community, and we started reaching hundreds of new people every week. This new space and its location gave us a much bigger platform to Love Our City. We did several outreaches in the community, but most of them were hosted at our location, as it was in the middle of the community, and everyone knew it as the old Toys' R' Us. We hosted food giveaways, block parties, back-to-school events, gifts at Christmas, and much more. We partnered with our local Community Development Corporation and helped start a program called Steps For Success that worked one-on-one with families in poverty to help them become self-sustainable. We coached close to a hundred families at our facility. Our church became widely known as a church that gave back to our community.

THE DISCONTENT & THE DREAM

But even with all of these great programs, I was still uneasy that we could do more. We had a few hundred people involved in doing outreach, but it was only about 20% of our church. We highlighted it on Sundays, showed videos, and encouraged people to get involved, but we couldn't get past a small percentage of our church doing the real work. We all know the 20/80 rule, but I was convinced that we could break that. I got inspired by a few other churches that seemed to have cracked the code. One of those churches was a church in Lansing, Michigan, that we had helped plant just a year before. I was super inspired to see them do this amazing serve week. I called Pastor Jerome Vierling, and he gave me the details, and I got fired up.

I prayed and waited about a month before I presented it to our leadership team. It was October 2016. I walked into the staff meeting with a big new vision. I said, "Guys... our outreach stuff is good, but what if we could make it amazing? We only have about 20% of our church involved, but what if we could more than double that?" Everyone was like... "uh, how?" I asked, "When do we generally do our outreaches?" In unison, everyone said, "Saturdays." I went on to explain, "Well, if you think about it, about 40% of our church family works on Saturdays. In addition, you have lots of families that have sporting events with their kids, some people travel on the weekends, and for others, it's their only day off, and they aren't leaving the house. That is a big reason why we only have 20% involved... most other people are already doing something. So we're going to expand the opportunities and give more options. Here is the big vision - 500 people serving at 50 different community service projects over the course of a week." Jaws dropped, and people gasped. "We never had 500 people serve at anything in the history of our church. That is more than half of our congregation." Someone else jumped in, "50 projects, what in the world would we do? I can only think of a couple."

I first addressed the question about having more than half of our church get involved. Our church already had outreach and evangelism in our DNA. It wasn't foreign. If we offered more time options, we would see more participation.

If we clearly cast the vision, I was fully confident that our people would rise to the occasion. Then I moved on to the second question and pulled out the whiteboard and drew a circle in the middle that represented the church. I said, "Who are the demographics that live in a three to five-mile radius of our church? Let's name them." I challenge you to do this with your leadership team and think about the variety of neighbors you have. Our team started rattling off the different people groups; College Students (we have the University of South Florida right up the street with 50,000 students), business people, health care workers (we're next to Florida's largest medical district), lower income families (93% of our immediate neighborhood is rental housing), Immigrants, Spanish speakers, homeless, senior citizens, teachers... We quickly had over a dozen demographics on the whiteboard. "Ok, now let's connect relevant projects to each one of those people groups."

Many of us will say that we want our church to love our neighbors, but those of us who have outreaches usually do only one main thing: give away free stuff to poor people. Of course, we need to do that. It's biblical. Most churches don't do enough of this. But is that all? My church was already crushing it at this, but I was feeling uncomfortable and started asking questions. What about middle-class people who don't need a backpack or a Turkey at Thanksgiving? What about affluent people who don't need any physical resources? They need

Jesus, too! And if we reach them, they can help us with more resources to reach lower-income people who do need them. But they have everything they need. How can we connect with them? Our team began to brainstorm the different types of projects that could reach the people groups on our list. We came up with three main categories of projects that I'll share later in the chapter.

PLANTING SEEDS

From those first meetings, our goal with Love Our City has always been to simply serve our neighbors with the love of Jesus and plant seeds. The purpose wasn't to preach at people, it was to let our actions do the preaching. Of course, we are looking for opportunities to pray with people and share the gospel if the situation presents itself, but with many of our neighbors, this is our first interaction. We're not trying to force anything on anyone. Each situation needs discerning leaders and volunteers. We're focused on building a relationship and getting to know them as we serve them. We are building bridges. There were no conditions for us to serve someone. They didn't have to look like us, believe like us, vote like us, or live like us... We showed them love simply because they are our neighbors. We also planted a seed by giving them a flyer and inviting them to come to the Love Our City party, which was on Easter Sunday, coming up the following week. Research shows that Easter Sunday is the biggest Sunday of the year, when people will say yes to a church invite. So we literally put all our eggs in the Easter basket. We put these flyers in the gift bags, and many times we personally hand them to someone that we're connecting with. The flyer is a two-sided flyer that has Easter on one side, and the Sunday after Easter is promoted on the other side. Our church intentionally always does a big Sunday the week after to try to get more people to come back and stick. For most churches, the Sunday after Easter is one of the lowest attended of the year, but for our church, it usually is the second largest attended. The Sunday after Easter, we'll feature a guest speaker or a guest artist and have something special, like Free Food or bounce houses. Some of the speakers and artists we've had over the years were Montell Jordan, KB, Christopher "Play" Martin, and Myron Golden. We also have a Water Baptism celebration the week after Easter to celebrate all the people who made decisions to follow Christ on Easter.

Shortly after that staff meeting about the new outreach vision, we announced to all our ministry leaders that we were going to do our first serve week called "Love Our City" coming up in the Spring of 2017. Everyone was excited, and we started planning out the framework of the rollout. Every year, we have a Vision Sunday in January to reveal our word for the year and what initiatives go along with it. That Sunday, we announced this exciting new thing coming in March called Love Our

City. Our leadership team wore T-Shirts with the new logo. We encouraged people to commit to give a special offering in early March to help us bless our community and provide for all the projects we would be doing together. People were excited, and hundreds of commitments came in over the following weeks. The big give day came in early March, and we raised close to $30,000 to pay for all the projects and free T-Shirts for everyone who participated. Remember my dream to have 500 people serve at 50 community service projects? Did we reach it? No, we actually exceeded it! We had over 600 people serve, and we had to add more projects. We ended up completing 72 community service projects that very first year, and we touched over 10,000 people in our neighborhood. It blew us away, and we knew we were onto something.

GROWTH OVER THE NEXT FEW YEARS

In our second year, we grew to have 1,000 people serve at over 100 projects. We flipped the paradigm and had over 80% of our church serve that week! By our third year, we felt confident to invite people from outside of our church to come and serve with us. We did this in a strategic way to make this another layer of outreach. The Sunday that we opened the sign-ups on the website, I asked the church, "How many of you have someone you've invited to church and they still haven't come?" Most of our church raised their hands. I said,

"I know a way you can possibly get them here! Invite them to come and serve with you at Love Our City! Tell them it's free and they get a free T-Shirt! Everyone loves a free T-Shirt!" I also stressed to them not to invite their friends who go to another church. We specifically wanted to invite people who didn't go to church. That year, we had over 100 people come and serve with us who didn't attend our church. The church is the home base where all the projects start. So they first had to come to the church to check in for their project, meet their leader, get their supplies, and get their free T-Shirt. Each project takes a group picture and does a quick prayer together before they leave for the serving location. These guests got to serve with their friend that invited them and also meet other people from the church. Most of them had never seen a church give back to the community like this, and it changed the narrative of what many of them thought about church. Everyone at the project is inviting people to come to the big party on Easter, and giving them an invitation card, and those outsiders get curious and also want to come. So we were reaching people we were serving, and also reaching some of the guests who were serving with us.

In the third year, we had close to 1,500 people serve with us at 152 projects. It was crazy! Being that we focused our projects in a 3-5 mile radius of the church, the impact was undeniable. That week, everywhere in Uptown Tampa you saw groups of people wearing their Love Our City shirts.

Our community became an Innovation District in 2015 and started an annual event called "The State of Uptown." Part of this event was the Community Impact Awards, where they gave out three awards to community partners. One for corporations, one for non-profits, and one for individuals. Love Our City won the non-profit award in 2018. In 2019, they asked me to be the host of the award portion of the event every year since then. It's been an honor to share the stage for ten minutes and host this segment in front of our mayor, city council, congressmen, and key business executives from our city. Love Our City grew the reputation of our church and changed the narrative about what many people think about churches. Love Our City has become a staple event in our city that people appreciate and support.

2020 was going to be our biggest year yet! We planned on continued growth and impact… and then the unexpected happened. The pandemic hit. We had to cancel Love Our City week as it was right at the beginning of the lockdown period due to COVID-19. Our team quickly pivoted and assessed the needs and shifted from doing a serve week to serving people every week for many months to come. We still loved our city, but it looked much different. As leaders, we need to be flexible and ready to change our plans depending on the needs at hand. Our church is in Florida, so every few years we have to deal with Hurricanes. We have systems in place so we are ready to respond when disaster hits. 2024 was our worst year as we were hit back-to-back with Hurricane Helene and then just days later, we got an even stronger Hurricane Milton. Power was out in over 75% of the county, but our church is in a commercial district with all power underground, so we still had power. We became a community hub and distribution point. The day after the storm, we opened up and fed over 500 hot meals and gave away pallets and pallets of supplies. Over the next few weeks, we served thousands of people at multiple events on the church property. Several families are part of our church today as we served them with relief efforts. How were we able to do so much? Partners!

THE POWER OF PARTNERS

Our church paid for the majority of the Love Our city costs in the first year. We casted vision and people gave to a special offering. Our team didn't try to get sponsors, as it was our first year doing it. We felt like we needed to have proof of concept and build a reputation before inviting outside sponsors and donors. Since then, partnerships and sponsors have been key to the growth of our impact. When the pandemic hit in 2020, we already had several established partnerships with great organizations in our city. We had trusted relationships. Some of them called us before we called them. They were asking us if we could partner with them. One of those first calls was from Feeding Tampa Bay. Our church used them to regularly supply our food pantry and Love Our City week. They were our partner who helped us give away a bag of groceries to thousands of homes. We purchased those groceries from them for pennies on the dollar. It was a blessing. When they called us at the beginning of the pandemic, they shared that most of the food pantries in the city were run by elderly people who were at risk, so they closed them. They knew we had a younger congregation and asked us if we could become a food distribution hub in our parking lot. We had an army of young volunteers, and we had the space. Our answer was Yes! But, the follow up question was how much will the food cost? They told us, "Don't worry about it, it's totally free!" They had the funding and just needed a trusted partner in our part of the city. We asked, "When can we start?" They said, "This Friday". We said, "Let's Go!" For six months, they dropped off a truck load of pallets that our volunteers sorted, and we gave groceries to 300 plus families every Friday. As the summer went on, most of our volunteers went back to work and it was getting harder to have our team to do everything. We were tired. God answered our prayer as they had another location at the University of South Florida close because school was starting back up. They wanted to combine that location with ours and send multiple tractor-trailers, staff, and volunteers. That took our grocery drive thru to 800 families every week. The impact grew, and it didn't cost us a penny.

We also had a partnership with our local business district that created a fund to buy hot meals from local restaurants to keep their employees working and use the food to feed families in need. They had funding and restaurants, but no connection to large groups of people. That's where we came in. We gave away thousands of hot meals at the grocery drive-thru in to-go boxes. We gave away thousands of hot meals at church services and events. It was a blessing to be a connector in the community to get the resources to the people who needed them most.

As I'm writing this, we have multiple amazing partnerships that provide us with unique ways to bless our community. Every month, we host a free Amazon store. One of our partners gives us a tractor-trailer with over twenty pallets of Amazon boxes with anything and everything you can imagine that is on their website. It's overstock items that include vacuums, trampolines, air fryers, juicers, pet items, furniture, electronics, and more. We set up our gym like a store, and families pre-register to come and shop. Everything is on sale for Free 99. Every family gets to pick three items for absolutely free. We also regularly take these items out to local apartment complexes and do a pop up blessing. This past summer, we partnered with an organization that gave us food boxes to distribute to lower-income families with children who got free lunches during the school year. Each week, we served over 150 families. This year, we started a new partnership with Publix, as they give us grocery items that are about to expire, and we quickly distribute them to families in need. I could go on and on about how partnerships have multiplied our impact. We have several families attending our church that have been touched by an outreach in the past six months. Our church is growing as our impact is growing.

What can a local partnership look like for your church or ministry? You have to be intentional to network and build relationships. We've met many of these organizations at local business meetings, trainings, and city meetings. We have also been connected through direct relationships with people in the church who knew someone at these organizations, or who work at the company. Don't be afraid to get out there and meet other people, and find out what they are doing. Share what you're doing and what you are dreaming about doing. We know we can't do everything, but we can all do something! It takes a network of churches, corporations, government, and non-profits to meet all the needs in our neighborhoods. We're not here to compete with other organizations or duplicate services. We can complement each other and work with each other's strengths. We also don't have to agree with everything a partner does in order to work with them. We find common ground, and we let our light shine for Christ in everything we do. Partnership is another key element that has changed the narrative in our community about the church.

CREATIVE PROJECTS TO SERVE YOUR NEIGHBORS

When our staff brainstormed fifty community service projects, it was very important that we identified someone to oversee the project. It clearly could not be me as the Lead Pastor. I cast the vision, I support it, and speak into it, but you must designate an organized point person. Visionary leaders need gifted administrators. I'm so grateful for Lily Perlaza and how she jumped in and made this dream become a reality. We all worked on the ideas and the framework, but she filled in all the details with logistics. She managed the projects, leaders, volunteers, budget, supplies, sponsors, and more! Lily thrived so much doing this that eventually it became her main role at the church. She fully transitioned into becoming our outreach director over Love Our City.

Our desire is to love all of our city and create projects and experiences to show the love of Jesus to all kinds of different demographics. We do this with a variety of community service projects that break down into three main categories. The first one is "Service Projects." These are sweat equity projects that include cutting someone's grass, painting a house, cleaning a yard, a school, or a city block. They even included going to a foster family's home and assembling furniture. These projects don't take a lot of money; they just require some helping hands to assist. They reach several demographics and also create space for conversations and ministry to take place.

The second category is pay it forward projects. This kind of project can actually reach all kinds of demographics. Let me give you some examples. Just around the corner from our church is an urban laundromat. We have built a relationship with the owner, and they allow us to come in and pay for everyone's laundry. If you haven't been to a laundromat lately, it has become expensive to wash your clothes. We show up with $500 of quarters, detergent, and fabric softener. This surprise makes the day of the people who are cleaning their clothes. Just next to that plaza is a Starbucks that attracts a totally different demographic. A lady got out of her new Mercedes, and some of our team walked up and gave her a gift bag and a gift card to pay for her coffee. She burst into tears. Our team talked with her and prayed with her to find out that she had been struggling with depression and was on the verge of a panic attack in her car. She prayed that God would give her a sign. Then she got out of her card and there we were blessing her. You can literally become the answer to someone's prayer! This lady didn't need us to buy her coffee (although we did); she needed someone to see her and pray with her. The laundromat and the Starbucks projects are just a few hundred feet apart, but they reach two totally different groups of people. Pay it forward projects can touch all kinds of people on your demographics list.

The third category of projects we do is Appreciation Lunches. We create appreciation lunches for teachers, firefighters, police officers, and health clinic workers in our district. We serve close to 1,000 catered lunches each Love Our City week. Each recipient also gets a gift bag with some goodies and an invitation card. This has helped us form great relationships in our neighborhood and open doors for us to serve schools in other ways. It has also led to some of these educators and first responders joining our church family. Assess what the demographics and needs are in your neighborhood, and you might create appreciation lunches for other groups. As you research and dream with your team, you may come up with several other categories of projects.

CREATING A NON-PROFIT

As Love Our City grew, we decided to create its own 501c3 non-profit that was separate from the church. We strategically registered it as a non-religious organization. A large portion of funding from the government, city, and corporations cannot be donated to a church or religious entity. In many cases, this is written into the bylaws of some corporations to protect themselves from being solicited by their employees. We registered Love Our City Tampa as a non-profit that offers services and resources to our community. It can still be run with Christian values if the officers choose to run it that way, so it doesn't restrict us from any outreach elements.

This designation has allowed us to receive several additional grants and build partnerships that would not have happened if it had to run through the church. As I am writing this, we just received our largest donation to date from a foundation that was closing its doors and needed to give it to another non-profit doing work in the community. We're not saying you have to separate it, but as your outreach efforts grow, it can be a great option to consider.

LOVE OUR CITY COFFEE

I love bringing people together. Around the time Love Our City was birthed, something else was also brewing inside me. God gave me this vision to create a coffee shop in our church lobby that would be open 7 days a week. This could actually work as our location is on a street that has 80,000 cars pass our building daily. It's a commercial district with lots of traffic. It would not only be a great amenity on Sundays before and after services for people to connect, but it would also create outreach opportunities all week. It would be a win-win on so many levels. We could create several jobs and a new revenue stream for the church. This coffee shop could help fund our outreach efforts! I was convinced we could get this done quickly, but it took years. We had a pandemic hit, permitting in our city radically changed, and there was a construction boom. And did I mention inflation? All of this and more stretched out the project years longer than expected. I almost gave up multiple times. It was hard. But anything that is going to have a huge impact is usually going to be harder than expected.

In 2025, we finally passed our final inspections and received our certificate of occupancy for the new second-floor mezzanine. We fully remodeled our lobby, and the space looks beautiful. It has a very modern, artsy vibe with epoxy marble floors, custom LED tube lighting, wood slot wall aesthetics, and lots of new glass. It's a wow factor when the community steps into our building. In 2026, we opened the shop first on Sundays and eventually during the week. We're still in the early stages of building this brand, but we're excited and confident that this will accomplish several things. It will continue to brand Love Our City in our community. It will be coffee with a cause. Every time someone buys coffee from us, they will be made aware that a portion of their purchase is going right back into our community. We have also made Love Our City coffee bags available for people to order from all over the world. We even have wholesale pricing for other churches and organizations to buy, so they can use it for fundraising for their outreaches. If you ever come to

Florida, you have to come get a cup of Love Our City coffee! You can order some coffee at www.loveourcitycoffee.com.

CREATING A MOVEMENT

We first launched this book that became a movement in 2018. You are holding the updated version in your hand. Along with the book, we created a physical leaders' box kit for church leaders to start Love Our City in their community. We've had over 350 churches get a physical box kit.

We have upgraded to a digital box kit that is now available. The beautiful thing is that we've found this outreach concept works in any context. We've had churches do it from rural environments, from the suburbs, and from the city. We've had churches with twenty members do it, and churches with five campuses participate. I have run into people at church conferences where I did workshops the year before, and they would thank me and tell me how they implemented it in their city.

One of my favorite Love Our City stories is from some churches in New York. My friend Pastor Joe Nieves from Transformation Church in Middletown, New York, implemented Love Our City and did several projects. He introduced me to his friend Pastor Jose Vazquez from Church at the Bridge in Newburg, New York. Joe told him he needed to plug in with Love Our City. Jose was already doing outreach events, but created a Love Our City serve week with a big event at the end of the week. He partnered with the city on several events, and they decided to adopt the *"Love Our City"* slogan and put it all over the city. It's amazing when you see a city embrace the movement and see the value of the local church. This is narrative changing! Both of these churches have continued to serve their communities in creative ways, and since the pandemic, have seen incredible growth, where both churches are now doing 3 services on Sundays.

 YOUR NEXT STEPS

Love our city is customizable to your context. We've had some churches start by doing three projects, while others had the capacity to do over one hundred. The leader's box kit includes a project template that gives you ideas for a few dozen different types of projects. It is laid out in a spreadsheet for you to fill in the details of how many people you need, how many it will reach, what the cost is, what supplies are needed, and more. The kit also includes a sermon series, small group video curriculum, artwork, a fundraising guide, and more. It is offered for free when a church purchases books. We believe this book is vital to help transform the hearts of your church family and take them from just doing a one-off community service project to it becoming a lifestyle.

Studying God's word together and learning the theology is transformational and creates incredible momentum when you do it churchwide. Get your books and digital box kit at **www.loveourcitybook.com**

DAY

OUR PROBLEM

"I know all the things you do, that you are neither hot nor cold. I wish that you were one or the other! But since you are like lukewarm water, neither hot nor cold, I will spit you out of my mouth!" — Revelation 3:15 NLT

"The system's so foul – got us thinking we need it / Work more, spend more, but the cycle's repeated…"

"APPRECIATE" - URBAN D. (UNORTHODOX ALBUM)

1

We are comfortable. We are very comfortable. We live in a culture with so many options and choices. Everything is literally available right at our fingertips. We order our food, our Uber, and our new kitchen sink right from our phone as we simultaneously stream videos and scroll our social media timelines. We are over-stimulated, over-stretched, and overwhelmed. We are busy in our comfort zone. Our vision is blurred. People are dying all around us, but we can only find the time to complain about our Wi-Fi being too slow.

Most of us want significance. We want to make a difference. Many of us want to "love our city, but most of us have little margin in our lives. Whatever space we have is quickly filled with trivial things that won't matter in the scope of eternity. We really want change, but we ourselves don't really want to change. In his book, Overrated, Eugene Cho drops a serious truth bomb, stating, "Most people are more in love with the idea of changing the world than actually changing the world." Ouch.

Our culture today is similar to the church in Laodicea. Jesus challenged their mindsets, allowing them to see that their lukewarm lifestyles would lead them to be spit out of his mouth. This is one of the most misquoted passages in the Bible. Revelation 3:15 reads, "I know all the things you do, that you are neither hot nor cold. I wish that you were one or the other! But since you are like lukewarm water, neither hot nor cold, I will spit you out of my mouth!" This verse is many times interpreted and preached that God wants us to be either hot or cold towards him. Be all the way in or all the way out. No half-stepping. No faking it. I've heard it preached like this multiple times. Back in the day, I believed this and even explained it like this myself. That can sound good, but that's far from the correct context.

Several years ago, I preached a message at my church on this passage called "The Lukewarm Bucket Challenge". At the beginning of the message, I read the verses you just read, and I asked the congregation a true or false question, "Do these verses mean God wants you to be either hot or cold towards him? It's all or nothing. Is that statement true or false?" I brought six people up on stage to take the challenge and seated them in chairs facing the crowd. If they answered it correctly, they would get a free T-shirt, but if they answered it wrong, they would get a bucket of lukewarm water poured on their heads. It was an intense moment. Our DJ was spinning some upbeat music, and the crowd was on the edge of their seats. Five out of six people got it wrong! So did we really pour a bucket of lukewarm water on people's heads at a church service? I'll get to that in a minute.

The Laodiceans in Revelation chapter 3 were wealthy and comfortable, just like most of us. The city of Laodicea was located in modern-day Turkey. It was a cosmopolitan city that was economically booming. They were crushing it! In fact, in 60 AD, there was a huge earthquake, and they refused any aid from the Roman government as they insisted they would rebuild everything with their own wealth. The people were very independent and prideful. But, even with all their money and their luxury, the Laodiceans had a problem. They were thirsty.

Have you ever been thirsty on a hot day? When my daughters were younger, they used to love theme parks here in Florida. And as any good dad would do, I sometimes found myself walking through the Florida heat to wait in long lines to get on roller coasters that give you a headache. Florida summers at the theme park are a lot of fun with 95 degree temperatures combined with 95 percent humidity! Have you ever gone up to a water fountain on a scorching day like that? You are hoping for a refreshing cold mouthful of water, but instead you end up getting lukewarm water with a nasty taste and smell to it? If so, you're not alone. I've experienced this multiple times at these theme parks I love so much. I think they strategically do this so you have to buy an $8 bottled water or a $10 soda, but that's another sermon for another book. Being thirsty on a hot summer day paints a familiar picture for us. None of us likes lukewarm water on a day like that. However, what this meant for the church in Laodicea was on another level. It painted a much more vivid picture than us standing at a lukewarm water fountain in the heat.

Even though Laodicea was a wealthy city, it had no fresh water source of its own. A smaller city called Hierapolis, which was six miles north, was known for its hot springs. People would travel from all over the Roman Empire to bathe in the hot springs of Hierapolis. It was known to heal people of certain illnesses. The hot water was useful for bathing, cooking, and washing clothes. That hot water had a purpose. To the south of Laodicea, there was a smaller city called Colossae. Paul had planted a church there and even wrote a letter in the New Testament to them called Colossians. Their city was blessed to have these cold springs with fresh, pure water for drinking.

The Laodiceans built pipelines, called aqueducts, to these cities north and south of them in order to supply fresh water to their city. Unfortunately, by the time the hot water traveled over six miles from Hierapolis to Laodicea, it was lukewarm and tasted foul due to the pipeline deposits floating in it. Similarly, when the fresh cold spring water traveled over ten miles from Colossae to Laodicea, it became lukewarm and carried a foul taste and smell.

When Jesus shares this illustration in Revelation 3 with the church of Laodicea, it carries a literal meaning as they constantly struggled with dirty lukewarm water. People would literally spit it out when they tasted it. The church of

1

Laodicea nauseated Jesus. They made Him so sick that He spat them out. The word spit in the English language does not begin to express the depth of Jesus' disgust for the church of Laodicea. The word used for "spit" in Revelation was originally written in Greek, "emeo," which means vomit!

So Jesus didn't mean I'd rather you be hot for me or cold for me… No, what He meant was, I would rather have you be useful for me. Hot water was useful. Cold water was useful. Lukewarm water was not useful for anything.

We want people to be useful for Jesus, and we want to teach them how to be useful for Jesus. But pouring lukewarm water on someone's head for answering a question wrong in church... that would be so wrong. When five out of six people got the question wrong regarding what Jesus meant about being Lukewarm, we had already come up with a plan. They were blindfolded and thought they were going to get water dumped on their head. Instead, as we built the anticipation and counted down from 3, 2, 1... they got a bucket full of tiny shredded paper pieces on their heads. The crowd laughed! Their blindfolds came off, and the people were relieved. A couple of the ladies didn't appreciate picking the shreds out of their hair, but at least they didn't get soaked.

The shredded paper had significance as an illustration. We can do a lot with a piece of paper. It can communicate a number of things as we print or write something on it. But when a piece of paper is shredded into thousands of little pieces, it becomes useless. When we are lukewarm, we can become useless. We can't fulfill the purpose God has for us.

Now remember, this passage of scripture wasn't written to everyone who lived in the city of Laodicea. It was a message specifically for the people in the church of Laodicea. If we're being honest, this letter could have easily been written to the people in the church of America today. So many people go to church, but overall, they are not living out their spiritual purposes. They are not allowing themselves to be useful for God to work in them and through them; And Jesus makes it very clear that those kinds of people make him sick.

LOVE LESSON:

God doesn't want us to be hot (all in) or cold (all out), he wants us to be useful! (Rev. 3:15)

LOVE QUESTION:

In what ways would you say that you are currently useful for God?

LOVE APPLICATION:

How can you apply this to your life?

LOVE NOTES:

What stuck out to you?

What else is God saying to you?

43

DAY

2

OUR WEALTH

"You say, 'I am rich. I have everything I want. I don't need a thing.' And you don't realize that you are wretched and miserable and poor and blind and naked." — Revelation 3:17 NLT

"I'll be honest, it was hard at first / Even though we say we want to put God first / Because we all struggle with this material thirst / But we can't take nothing when we get in the hearse"

"GIVE, MULTIPLY, GROW, REPEAT"- URBAN D. (LOVE OUR CITY ALBUM

esterday, we discussed our comfort and examined Revelation 3, where Jesus emphasized that He wants us to be useful to Him. But, wait... there's more! Jesus says additional things to the church in Laodicea that also apply to us. Verse 17 shows us that the extremely wealthy people claimed they didn't need anything from anyone. Even when a major earthquake struck, they refused any aid from the Roman Government. It was because they had this prideful vibe of "We got this!" But Jesus tells them that they are oblivious to the fact that spiritually they are pitiful, blind, and homeless. They were living in deception. They thought they were something that they were not.

Have you ever met someone like that? There once was a lady who came up to her pastor and told him, "I have a sin, and I need your help. I come to church every Sunday, and I can't help thinking I'm the prettiest girl in the congregation. I know I shouldn't think like that. I want you to help me conquer this sin." The pastor looked at her and smiled and said, "Child, don't worry about it, in your case it's not a sin, you're just horribly mistaken." Many of us have some funny stories of people living in deception. But at the end of the day, there are so many people that think they are good and that "they got this", but the reality is that they are the total opposite. Similarly, the people of Laodicea thought they were all good, but they weren't.

Most of you reading this are living in one of the richest countries in the world today. America has the most wealth and the most advanced civilization in the history of mankind. I know most of us don't feel rich, but we are. We are filthy rich! I'm not talking about some religious talk about being spiritually rich. I'm talking about real monetary wealth. We don't feel this way as we live in a hyper-consumer culture, which is always pushing something new to buy, to experience, or to eat. But let me break down some facts. Nearly half of the world lives on less than $6.85 a day. [1] If you check out the website **www.givingwhatwecan.org**, and scroll down to the section that tells you how rich you are, you can see where you rank. The median household income in the United States in 2024 was $83,730. [2] At that amount you would be richer than over 88% of people in the world. We may not go around saying, "We are rich," like the Laodiceans did, but on a global scale, we are very rich. Most of us are actually richer than they were and have access to cleaner water and better wi-fi than they did (They had neither).

Jesus gave the Laodiceans a prescription to go from self-reliance to total dependence on God. Jesus told them they needed to buy three things. They couldn't go to the bougie Beverly Hills Mall of Laodicea, and they couldn't get it from Amazon Prime. They could only get it directly from Jesus. In verse 18, Jesus says, "I advise you to buy gold from me, gold that has been purified by fire. Then you will be rich." Laodicea

was one of the richest cities in ancient history. Many people could afford to buy anything they wanted. But here God is saying that they needed spiritual riches through faith in Christ. He talks about gold that has been purified by fire. Earthly riches that we have will burn up, but spiritual wealth has eternal value; that's why the last part of the verse says, "then you will be rich." Jesus then tells them the second thing to buy from him is white garments. Those white garments represent spiritual purity. One of the biggest sources of wealth in Laodicea was garments. Their specialty was black wool cloth. This was the signature product that made them rich and famous in the Roman Empire. Their prosperity was also due to their well-known eye ointment. People came from all over the region to get treated at their famous eye clinic and school. So here is Jesus making this analogy that they need to get this third thing from him, to buy eye ointment for your eyes so you will be able to see. This spiritual eye ointment would help them open up their vision to their sins so they would see the truth and ask God for forgiveness.

Even though thousands of years and thousands of miles separate us from the Laodiceans, we have a lot more in common than we think. Most of us have access to buy whatever we want right from our smartphones. Because of their wealth, the Laodiceans had whatever luxuries of their day were available. Although we may not feel rich, we are extremely wealthy compared with the rest of the world.

But the material things we have will get old, worn out, and eventually go out of style.

Jesus said, "Where your treasure is, there your heart will be also. So, we have to ask ourselves: What are we constantly working towards? What is the treasure we are going after? If we are honest, our main focus isn't always working on our spiritual wealth. Many of us are thinking about financial wealth. We're focused on bills we are trying to pay off, a vacation we are saving for, a new toy we want, or something we need to buy the kids. The list seems to never end. I know this firsthand as a husband and father with two daughters. It's easy to forget how blessed we are and to forget about our responsibility to use it in ways to have an eternal impact.

LOVE LESSON:

We are much richer than we think. Where much is given, much is required.

LOVE QUESTION:

How could we be more eternally productive with the wealth that we have?

LOVE APPLICATION:

How can you apply this devotional to your life?

LOVE NOTES:

What stuck out to you?

What else is God saying to you?

DAY 3

OUR PRESCRIPTION

"I correct and discipline everyone I love. So be diligent and turn from your indifference." — Revelation 3:19 NLT

"Our soul lives on after we leave this earth / And the Bible promises heaven to those who have a spiritual rebirth / With Jesus / He comforts us – He frees us / So the best is yet to come – it's gonna get better / I'll see you soon fam – cuz we're gonna live forever!"

"ETERNAL" - URBAN D. (LOVE OUR CITY ALBUM)

I need to regularly remind myself, and my girls, that all these earthly things are just temporary, but the spiritual things are eternal. And I'm a Pastor! But I know I'm not alone in this. We can all struggle with our vision at times. God gives us a prescription for our lenses, just like he gave the Laodiceans a prescription in this passage. We know this prescription is good for us. We know it will help us see clearly. We know it will help us avoid all kinds of headaches. However, we think the non-prescription sunglasses that the culture offers are cooler. They are constantly advertised to us, and it seems like other people wearing them are having an amazing time. So we end up putting them on at times to fit in. It seems so normal. From time to time, we'll put on our God-prescribed lenses when we go to church, in front of our parents, and in front of other Christians we want to impress. The truth is, wearing them occasionally doesn't correct the overall direction of our vision.

In 2017, I lost my father and my mother in the same year. Their lives and their ministry touched countless people who were changed forever. I am so grateful for their example, and I know they are with the Lord. My dad was sick for close to seventeen years, so his passing was closure for our family; nonetheless, it is still super hard to lose your dad. My mom was always the life of the party and made friends everywhere she went. She loved people, and she loved to talk. When she was healthy, saying goodbye on the phone was always a challenge because she just kept going and going. The last few months of her life, I was lucky just to keep her on the phone for four or five minutes because she had lost most of her energy. I've cried many tears, and I miss my parents like crazy, but I have a hope-filled, eternal perspective. The Bible consistently presents hope as a confident expectation about what is going to happen in the future. Hope is one of our deepest virtues as Christians. We are supposed to be hopeful people. We should find joy in hope, boast in hope, hold strong to our hope, overflow with hope, and even defend our hope. We go through trials because trials produce character, which in turn produces hope. People in our communities are desperate for hope. We are supposed to be hope pushers!

What is the object of our hope? God! We hope in God because of who he is, what he has done, and what he is going to do in the future. In Titus 1:1-2, Paul told Titus, "Paul, a servant of God and an apostle of Jesus Christ to further the faith of God's elect and their knowledge of the truth that leads to godliness - in the hope of eternal life, which God, who does not lie, promised before the beginning of time." In Acts 24:14-15, Paul was defending himself before Felix in Caesarea and said, "But I admit that I follow the Way, which they call a cult. I worship the God of our ancestors, and I firmly believe in the Jewish law and everything written in the prophets. I have the same hope in God that these men have, that he will raise both the righteous and unrighteous." Paul

3

even said in Corinthians that if there was no resurrection of Christ, we were all hopeless. Creation longs to be freed from its bondage to corruption and futility. If you watch the news, you are reminded of how divided our world is from politics, to policy, to religion, to race. It seems hopeless. Christ followers look forward to a new heaven and a new earth where we are in the presence of God. This is our blessed hope. This is the hope that causes us to love our city.

As an artist, one of the ways I deal with pain is by creating. I wrote a spoken word piece about losing my mom and my dad in the same year. I have written hundreds of songs, and it is by far the most emotional one I have ever penned. It passionately shares my pain, my perspective, and my hope. We created a music video for "Eternal," and it has touched tens of thousands of people. You can watch it here: (QR code) Additionally, I also launched a clothing line called "Eternal" that has the tag line "Live Forever" (www.eternal.clothing). My hope is not in my temporary time here on this sin-sick planet. My hope is ignited in my eternal perspective when I think about how we will live forever in God's presence in a place without sorrow, pain, or death.

We can correct our vision problem if we change our lens, lean in, and focus on the bigger picture. We know everything here is temporary, but if we can learn to operate and prioritize from this perspective, it will change the game. We can't take any of our material things with us. The only thing we can take with us into the next life is people. For the last few months that my mom was alive, there was a parade of people coming to visit her: neighbors, friends from work, friends from church, and friends from out of town. My Facebook feed was filled with so many comments from people sharing about what my mom meant to them. My mother was always full of hope and positivity. She loved God and loved people. She loved her city.

What mark will you leave behind after you breathe your last breath? Will you be known as someone who loved your stuff or someone who loved people?

"AT THE END OF THE DAY, PEOPLE WON'T REMEMBER WHAT YOU SAID OR DID; THEY WILL REMEMBER HOW YOU MADE THEM FEEL."
– MAYA ANGELOU

LOVE LESSON:

The only thing we can take with us to heaven is people.

LOVE QUESTION:

How are you trying to bring people with you to heaven?

LOVE APPLICATION:

How can you apply this devotional to your life?

LOVE NOTES:

What stuck out to you?

What else is God saying to you?

LOVE our City

DAY

4

OUR GOSPEL

I passed on to you what was most important and what had also been passed on to me. Christ died for our sins, just as the scriptures said. He was buried, and he was raised from the dead on the third day, just as the scriptures said." — 1 Corinthians 15:3-4 NLT

"But, I'm talking about a dangerous that's good / The kind of dangerous that can change your hood / And this ain't no gentrification / I'm talking about divine transformation / That's followed up by sanctification / Tranzlation / You become dangerous - just like him!

DANGEROUS JESUS

"DANGEROUS JESUS" - URBAN D.

ospel simply means Good News. There are lots of people in the world promoting what they think is good news, but it is not our gospel. They are promoting other religions, philosophies, ways to make money, and more. The differences are easy to spot. But there are also countless people sharing a false version of our gospel. There are two big problems with this: many of these people sincerely think they are spreading the correct gospel. They were taught incorrectly, and they are convinced they are right.

The other big problem is that most Americans are Biblically illiterate, so they don't know how to spot a false gospel. If it sounds good and the delivery is passionate or the social media post is edited well, it can seem right to them. So many people operate by feelings instead of facts. This is nothing new. False gospels were one of the biggest issues in the early New Testament church.

In some of Jesus last words, he told us to go and make disciples of all nations (Matthew 28:19). The gospel was clearly for everyone. But one of the early false gospels they had to fight against was legalism. A group of Jewish leaders was trying to get non-Jewish people (Gentiles) to conform to their cultural customs and laws to become real Christians. Paul confronted this in Galatians 2:21, where he said, "If keeping the law could make us right with God, then there was no need for Christ to die." That battle has been settled, but the legalistic gospel is still alive and well today. There are churches and cultures that have their own set of man-made traditions that they weave together with the gospel. Many of you reading this may have been turned off, like I was, by those man-made preferences and rules that churches added to the gospel. This has turned so many people away from God.

Another false gospel they fought against is the prosperity gospel, where people are taught that spiritual devotion is guaranteed to result in financial blessings. This is still popular in many circles today. This false gospel has damaged lots of people who bought into those promises, and when they didn't come true, they walked away from the church. The opposite of that is the poverty gospel, where people believe you have to be poor in order to be holy.

One of the biggest false gospels we are facing right now is the political gospel. The past decade has woven Christianity and politics together more than at any time during my life. This is dangerous, as many Christians are taking sides. It's becoming an us-versus-them battle. When you start to live like that, it becomes really difficult to love your neighbor if they don't vote like you.

We live in a cancel culture where people are quick to unfriend you if you don't agree with their candidate. Unfortunately, some Christians have joined in with this. How

can we be salt and light to the world if we are arguing and fighting with them on social media? I'm not saying we can't stand up for what we believe, but many are doing it in a hateful way that is not Christlike. We must be strategic in how we engage our community. The scripture says they will know us by our love for one another, not our politics.

So what is the true gospel? First, let me remind you what it is not. Our gospel is not self-improvement, moralism (be better), political ideology, prosperity, comfort, or Jesus + everything else. Today's verses of the day at the top of this devotional sum up what our gospel is (go back and read it again). This is the non-negotiable core. We are all sinners, sin separates us from God, and we can't save ourselves. Our gospel solves these problems.

The gospel is not a method; it is a person. Jesus! Jesus is fully God, fully man, and he is the only mediator between our heavenly Father. The work of the gospel was accomplished by Jesus once and for all. He died for us (substitutionary death). He paid for our sins in full (Atonement). Death was defeated when he rose on the third day (Resurrection). Jesus reigns as Lord (Jesus is King!).

Our gospel is offered freely, but it demands a response; Turn from sin and self-rule (Repentance & Submission to Jesus' leadership), and Trust Jesus alone for salvation (Faith). For those who believe we are declared righteous (Justification). We become part of God's family (Adoption). We are spiritually born again (Regeneration). We continually become more like Jesus (Sanctification). We will have eternal life and a future resurrection (Glorification). Our gospel is truly the best news our world has ever heard. We must find creative ways to share it with our lives, our actions, and our words.

LOVE LESSON:

The gospel is the good news that Jesus Christ lived, died, and rose again to save sinners by grace alone, through faith alone, for God's glory alone.

LOVE QUESTION:

When was the last time you shared the gospel with someone?

LOVE APPLICATION:

How can you apply this devotional to your life?

LOVE NOTES:

What stuck out to you?

What else is God saying to you?

LOVE
our City

DAY

OUR REVIVAL

"Now repent of your sins and turn to God, so that your sins may be wiped away. Then times of refreshment will come from the presence of the Lord, and he will again send you Jesus, your appointed Messiah." — Acts 3:19-20 NLT

"Infiltrating commercial districts and residential zones / Lyrically breathing new life in our culture's dry bones / invisible skin tones / From a cornea that scopes all people / waiting for a restoration for my people / like my man Ezekiel / Check the 37th chapter..."

"SPITTING SCRIPTURES"- URBAN D. FEAT. LOS 1 (UNHEARD ALBUM)

5

n church history, there have been several revivals and movements that have shaped culture. The very first one happened in the Roman Empire between the first and third century where Christianity exploded from a small Jewish movement into a global faith. It happened under persecution, not comfort. There were Celtic revivals in the 5th - 7th century. One of the most well known was the Protestant Reformation in the 1500's. This sparked massive renewal and reform that changed theology, education, politics, and culture. In the 1700 and 1800's, there were the great awakenings. In the early 1900's, there was the Azusa Street Revival in Los Angeles. This was a racially integrated revival with emphasis on the Holy Spirit, healings, and worship.

The Jesus Movement swept America in the 1960's and 70's. This brought hippies and counter-culture youth to Jesus. It helped launch contemporary Christian music. [1] Every generation prays for revival. Many revivals from the past have a pattern. Almost every major revival includes prayer before power. Repentance before renewal. Ordinary people before famous leaders. Social impact after spiritual awakening. Revival doesn't start with crowds; it starts with consecration.

I've been on this planet for over five decades. I grew up in the church and have been in ministry for over three decades. I've seen a lot. During my lifetime, there have been some movements that made an impact, and there have been some revivals at different churches here in America. But, overall, those things did not shape culture, as the number of people attending church and truly following Jesus has declined over the majority of my life. Yes, there have been some churches that are growing, thriving, and making an impact. There have been lots of bright spots and miracles. Yet overall, the church has continued to decline year after year. But in the past two years, something has been shifting. The decline has plateaued and started moving in the other direction.

According to barna.com's latest data, 66% of all U.S. adults say they have made a personal commitment to Jesus. That marks a 12% increase since 2021. Barna says, "The shift is not only statistically significant - it may be the clearest indication of meaningful spiritual renewal in the United States." [2] Among the biggest drivers of this resurgence are younger generations of Gen Z and Millennials. Surprisingly, younger men are driving this trend. For the first time in decades, younger adults are now the most regular churchgoers, outpacing older generations, who once formed the backbone of church attendance (We are seeing this at our church in Tampa). Another interesting stat is that many people are open to spirituality and Jesus, but hesitant to embrace organized religion or even identify as a Christian. [3]

5

Some of the biggest social media influencers on TikTok, Instagram, and YouTube are now Christians. They are putting out spiritual content that is regularly going viral. The Associated Press reported that streams of new music have been down the past year except for one genre: Christian music. [4] In 2025, Christian artist Forrest Frank surpassed mainstream artist Drake in the amount of monthly streams. [5] Several Christian songs recently landed in the Billboard Hot Top 40. In 2023, there was a revival at Asbury University and Auburn University that sparked the UniteUS movement, which has gone to dozens of universities and seen thousands come to Jesus and get baptized.

The Bible App YouVersion hit 1 billion downloads in 2025. They normally see a spike in downloads and opens in January and around Easter, but in 2025, they set records nearly every single month for the highest engagement. Brenna Connor, an industry analyst at Circana BookScan, told RNS in an email. "2024 marked a 20-year high for Bible sales in the U.S., and 2025 is on track to surpass these levels, underscoring the growing interest in religious content among U.S. consumers." [6] Personally, I can celebrate that our church had a record amount of salvations and over 300 baptisms in 2025. It was our biggest year of impact.

All of this data is exciting and encouraging, but does it mean we are in revival? I believe God is definitely moving and something is shifting, but we're not in a national revival yet. Could we be headed there? Only God knows, but I believe what we do as believers in this moment is critical. People are becoming more open to Jesus than they have in decades. It is an opportunity to rebrand the church as we love our city and show our neighbors who Jesus really is. We can't create revival, but we can position ourselves for spiritual renewal. God does the reviving as we seek him. Remember the patterns of true revival in history? Prayer, repentance, and social impact. Let's pray, let's repent for what we've done wrong, and let's serve our community in new ways. If we want real revival, these are vital spiritual renewal elements. You can't get around it. You can't hype it up. You can't get celebrities to co-sign it. Simply pray, repent, and serve.

LOVE LESSON:

True Revival starts with prayer, repentance, and ordinary people. It is followed up by social impact.

LOVE QUESTION:

What signs of spiritual renewal
have you seen around you?

LOVE APPLICATION:

How can you apply this devotional to your life?

LOVE NOTES:

What stuck out to you?

What else is God saying to you?

DAY

6

OUR CITIES

"Yes, I try to find common ground with everyone, doing everything I can to save some." — 1 Corinthians 9:22b NLT

"Imagine a new life, a new fam, a new city / Imagine a place with no political committee / Just lots of love, daps and high fives / Romans 6:4 in action – living new lives"

"NEW LIFE, NEW FAM, NEW CITY" - URBAN D. FEAT. JAY CABASSA (REBUILD ALBUM)

6

We live in an era of unprecedented human mobility. Our cities and metropolitan areas are rapidly changing and growing at a pace like never before. More than 80 per cent of people worldwide now live in towns and cities, according to a major United Nations report, and this figure is set to rise further, underscoring the need to ensure urban areas benefit both our health and the planet [1]. More and more people are clustering in metropolitan areas, and there is evidence that this trend will continue. The United Nations and the International Organization for Migration both estimated that around 3 million people move to cities every week [2]. That is close to 430,000 people every day, nearly 18,000 every hour. Our cities are not just quickly growing; they are also becoming more and more diverse in age, ethnicity, culture, and class. All these different worlds are converging in our cities. One single block could represent four generations, with over a dozen languages spoken, with million-dollar condos on one side of the street and section eight housing on the other.

Although the white population is moving back into the cities at rates we haven't seen in decades, they are no longer the majority. According to the US Census, white people made up 53% of the population in cities in 1990. By 2010, that number dropped to 41%. By 2020, that number dropped to 36%. Meanwhile, the Hispanic population during that same period of time grew from 17% up to 30%, and the Asian population grew from 5% to 10%. Surprising the African American population also fell in cities from 24% to 19% [3]. We could easily think that more white people moved to the suburbs. But, the suburbs have also grown much more diverse as well. In 1990, white people made up 81% of the suburban population, but this dropped to 65% by 2010. The Hispanic, Asian, and African American populations all grew substantially in the suburbs during this same time period. We can see that metropolitan areas as a whole are becoming more and more diverse. 2014 was the first year that more than 50% of children under the age of five were minorities. Many school districts in metropolitan areas are now becoming majority minority (students are non-white) [4]. Between fall 2012 and fall 2022, the percentage of public school students who were Hispanic increased from 24 to 29 percent. The percentage of public school students who were White decreased from 51 to 44 percent, and the percentage of students who were Black decreased from 16 to 15 percent [5].

This is a huge opportunity for Christ-followers, yet a huge challenge for many of them and the churches they are a part of. The days of going to a church where everyone looks like you are fading. Not just in our cities, but in the suburbs as well. A mono-ethnic church doesn't make sense in much of our current reality, and it certainly doesn't in our future. Faith Communities Today did a massive survey and reported that multi-ethnic churches have now grown to make up 25% of

American churches. Just twenty-five years ago, less than 12% of American churches were multi-ethnic [6]. That is more than double. The church as a whole still has a long way to go in order the match the diversity of our communities, but there is a shift happening. I have been part of the Multi-ethnic church movement and have spoken at several conferences and helped produce resources for churches. The bottom line is we cannot approach outreach and evangelism the same way we did decades ago when things were less diverse.

Every city is different. I have the opportunity to travel regularly to different places to speak, train, and consult. I see lots of similarities and differences in each city. Every city has some neighborhoods that are defined by race or certain ethnic groups. But many cities have more and more neighborhoods that are becoming diverse. I've lived in Tampa, Florida, for over thirty years, and although there are some areas that are more defined by ethnicity, many areas of the city and suburbs are diverse. Surprisingly, some of Tampa's suburban neighborhoods are actually even more diverse than parts of the city.

Our cities and suburbs have shifted even more since the pandemic. Many of the cities with extended lockdowns experienced a mass exodus as people fled to places with more freedom and warmer temperatures. New York City lost close to half a million people between 2020 and 2022. Some of those people fled to their suburbs, but many of them came to Florida. Tampa experienced a massive surge of people during the pandemic that changed our city forever. Our housing prices have doubled, along with our traffic. Over 50% of my church is new to our city since 2020. Over 95% of our church is not originally from Tampa. Many cities in the Southern part of the U.S. have experienced huge shifts. Our city and county have become more ethnically diverse and, at the same time, shifted politically to become more conservative. Some cities have seen the opposite shift since the pandemic. You must pay attention and notice the changes in your community so you can learn how to best reach your neighbors with the love of Jesus.

LOVE LESSON:

Our cities and suburbs are becoming more diverse in age, culture, class, and ethnicity.

LOVE QUESTION:

In what ways have you noticed your city changing?

LOVE APPLICATION:

How can you apply this devotional to your life?

LOVE NOTES:

What stuck out to you?

What else is God saying to you?

DAY 7

OUR REBUILD

"But now I said to them, 'You know very well what trouble we are in. Jerusalem lies in ruins, and its gates have been destroyed by fire. Let us rebuild the wall of Jerusalem and end this disgrace." — Nehemiah 2:17 NLT

"Rebuilding can knock the wind out of us / Kinda like a sucker punch hits straight to your gut / Nehemiah – had the physical rubble / Plus the spiritual rubble / Plus the outside opposition and trouble / Shallow breaths on the double / Trust me… I had more than a couple"

"BREATHING ROOM" - URBAN D. FEAT. THI'SL (REBUILD ALBUM)

7

n 2010, the church I lead relocated to an abandoned Toys R'Us building on Fowler Avenue and retrofitted a 43,000 square foot building. The area of North Tampa was nicknamed "Suitcase City" due to its high eviction rate, homelessness and transient nature. Fowler Avenue was dotted with lots of vacant retail and restaurant buildings that had thrived. The Great Recession hit our city hard, and many businesses that survived were fleeing to the new mall and retail areas that were opening in the suburbs. This was a forgotten part of the city. It was risky to invest millions of dollars in an old retail box and put a church there. But we knew God wanted us to rebuild this community and bring the love of Christ. I share the details of the miracle story of our church getting into the building in my book "Rebuild". We made it our goal to rebuild the neighborhood on the Nehemiah model: physically, spiritually, emotionally, and economically.

We had this vision that the neighborhood would look different over the next decade as we rebuilt it. This seemed like a lofty goal considering the stats. Shortly after we moved there one of our partners The University Area Community Development Corporation did a massive survey in our zip code and found the unemployment rate to be over 25%. The rental rate for housing was at 94%. Crime was over 100 times higher than other parts of the city. It looked bleak.

Loving a transient community is not easy. We ministered to many families, discipled them, and helped them get stable... and then they moved away. Then there were some that had a poverty mentality where they didn't want to do anything to change their situation, but they would gladly take whatever you were offering for free. Others didn't want to take anything, as they didn't trust anyone. Loving your city takes time. Building a reputation takes time. Seeing real results takes time. But, years into it, we were seeing some solid change. We had planted a lot of seeds and they were beginning to grow. Thousands of people had started a relationship with Jesus at our outreaches and church services. We baptized thousands of people since we've been in the former Toys 'R' Us. (Fun Fact: We baptized actor/rapper Christopher "Play" Martin from Kid N Play the day we hit 1,000 baptisms!) There were hundreds of families touched through our mentoring programs and discipleship classes. The spiritual landscape was being impacted. People were moving forward as they experienced the love of Christ and began loving others around them.

In 2015, there were some big physical shifts that began to happen in our neighborhood. It was designated an innovation district. Although there are rough neighborhoods, it also includes the University of South Florida with over 50,000 students, several research hospitals, the second largest VA hospital in the country, and several other large anchor businesses. Just a few miles east of the church, the district includes the Busch Gardens theme park, which attracts millions of tourists each year. The anchor tenants got together with the city, county, and business community and started a district to revitalize the area and change the reputation.

In April of 2016, Crossover Church was invited to some meetings by an outside firm that was studying our community to provide recommendations for its revitalization. We were invited to the meeting as they considered us an anchor tenant, and they wanted our input. We were the only church sitting at the table of about twenty major community businesses and institutions. At the meeting, I met Mark Sharpe, the director of the Innovation District. He was a former county commissioner, and he was excited to connect. We met at the church a few weeks later, and he invited me to be on the Advisory Board of the Innovation District. The board consisted mostly of CEO's and business leaders. Most others had to financially contribute to be on the board, but Mark said he wanted me involved because I understood the community and would help shape the way the board would invest its resources in neighborhood redevelopment. I was humbled, honored, and thankful for the invitation. It was a fulfillment of the rebuilding plan that God had put on our hearts many years before. In 2017, I was voted to become vice-chair of the board, specifically over community engagement.

I served for many years on the board to help bring needed changes to our community.

Over a decade into the rebuilding, our neighborhood got a new name: Uptown! Our church even painted a mural on the front of our building with the word Uptown as the centerpiece, with images from our city. We have watched our neighborhood improve. Unemployment has dropped. The eight-lane road that our church sits on now has very few vacancies. Spouts Grocery Store and Starbucks moved in down the block, along with several new businesses and restaurants. The former mall has been rebranded as "Rithm" and is undergoing a one billion dollar development project. Thousands of new apartments have been built for student housing. Several new stores and restaurants have been built. This is amazing, but there is still much work to be done. We still have an affordable housing crisis in our community, and we still have a homeless crisis that needs attention. We don't want gentrification to push people out, but create new opportunities for our current residents to be part of the rebuild. Our church continues to be involved in the community transformation, as we have loved our city for so many years. We've built trust and credibility to sit at the table. We've seen so many lives get changed. The problems we face are big, but the God we serve is bigger! We believe the best is yet to come!

LOVE LESSON:

Loving your city takes time. Building a reputation takes time. Seeing real results takes time. People are worth it!

LOVE QUESTION:

How is your church involved in your community? What are new ways you could influence the culture around you?

LOVE APPLICATION:

How can you apply this devotional to your life?

LOVE NOTES:

What stuck out to you?

What else is God saying to you?

LOVE
our City

LOVE our City WEEK 1 VIDEO SERIES

PLAY VIDEO

"'You must love the Lord your God with all your heart, all your soul, and all your mind.' This is the first and greatest commandment. A second is equally important: 'Love your neighbor as yourself.' The entire law and all the demands of the prophets are based on these two commandments."
— Matthew 22:37-40 NLT

▷ WE ALL HAVE SOME PROBLEMS...

1. We have a _____ Problem.

"Therefore, go and make disciples of all the nations, baptizing them in the name of the Father and the Son and the Holy Spirit. Teach these new disciples to obey all the commands I have given you. And be sure of this: I am with you always, even to the end of the age." — Matthew 28:19-20 NLT

* They were _____ by the Holy Spirit and He helped them get past their comfort issues.

* When we step out of our comfort zone God can empower us in _____ ways to reach our neighbors.

2. We have a _____ Problem.
(pic of Sunglasses and regular glasses)

3. We have a _____ Problem.

DISCUSSION QUESTIONS

1. How busy are you on a scale of 1-10
(1 being not busy and 10 being very busy)?

1   2   3   4   5   6   7   8   9   10

2. What are some things that keep you so busy that it can
be challenging to put God first and love your neighbor?

How can applying "Love your neighbor as you love
yourself" take you out of your comfort zone?

Peter was previously very uncomfortable admitting
he even knew Jesus. Now he was able to stand up
and preach to thousands. Read Acts 2:14-41.

4. Have you ever had God use you in a supernatural way?

5. What neighbors are difficult to see in a positive way?

6. What things do you see rapidly changing
around you (getting disrupted)?

7. How could you, your small group, and your
church respond to the disruption and reach
people in creative new ways in your city?

DAY

OUR HARVEST

"So pray to the Lord who is in charge of the harvest; ask him to send more workers into his fields." — Matthew 9:38 NLT

"But I love those who are optimistic / That could see our hood in Tampa and envision and innovation district / Helping people that are misfits / Find the God-given purpose of their existence"

"FRAMES" - URBAN D.

When most Christ-followers think about missions, they think about going to a third world country on a "missions trip". Evangelical Christianity in the West has traditionally focused more on "the ends of the earth" than on "Jerusalem." Many Christ-followers find it easier to go somewhere foreign and "love a city", than to go somewhere familiar and "love their city". But this is changing, as Millennials and Gen Z want to serve more and more in their own backyards. They see the need in front of them, and they want to engage and be hands-on.

In Matthew chapter 9, Jesus sees the needs in front of him, but he sees them with different eyes than his disciples. The scripture tells us that Jesus felt deep compassion for them. He saw their physical needs and even healed many of them from diseases and illnesses. Even greater, he saw their spiritual needs. Jesus used the metaphor that the people were like sheep lost without a shepherd. Then he switches metaphors and says the harvest is great, but the workers are few. The harvest and the workers show God's "need" met by man: God uses people to minister to other people.

God planted you in the city where you live now. It's your Jerusalem. Many of you may not originally be from there, but that is where you are now. Legendary Hip-Hop artist Rakim wrote a classic lyric that resonates with this: "It ain't where you're from, it's where you're at!" (1) Most of my childhood was spent growing up in the Philadelphia area. I loved my city. I loved the sports teams, the culture, the music, the graffiti, the soft pretzels, and of course, the greasy cheese steaks. I had family, friends, and a close church family. There was a lot of history, roots, and deep relationships.

Back in the day, I would have told you I would live in Philly for the rest of my life. But sometimes God has totally different plans for us, and he transplants us elsewhere. I've now been in Tampa, Florida, for over three decades. Tampa is my home. My community. My people. Tampa is my responsibility. My family is invested here, and my church has deep roots in our city. You have to choose to bloom where God has planted you... or transplanted you. Tampa would not have been my first choice, but now that I've been entrenched in it for so many years, I'm so grateful God brought me here. I love my city.

Our harvest is all around us in our own cities. There are people who are ripe to respond to the gospel, but there are not enough people living it out and sharing it in a credible way that connects. Jesus said pray for more workers for the harvest. If we begin to seek God and pray, many times we'll find out we are part of the solution to reach that ripe harvest right down the block. The Greek word kairos means "opportunity", "season", or "fitting time". In Jesus' day, an appointed time was expressed as kairos. The New Testament refers to eighty-six kairos opportunities. Jesus gave a very specific prayer request as he instructed the church to pray during a kairos moment.

This prayer request in Matthew 9 came after Jesus healed a man with leprosy, a Roman soldier's servant, spoke truth about the Kingdom of Heaven, healed Peter's mother-in-law, calmed a storm, cast demons out, healed a paralyzed man, and had dinner with a tax collector that the Pharisees referred to as scum. Did I mention he also raised a dead girl back to life? So you can see that Jesus was pretty busy. In that moment, he looked out into a crowd of people, and he saw a great need, and he called his people to action. He sees opportunities, he sees potential, he sees unfinished stories, but he sees a problem with this kairos moment as well.

How do you look at your life's story? The culture tells us - It's your life. You own it. You keep it. You do whatever you want, but yet, the scripture tells us - My life is part of God's big story. My story is part of this community, my family, and my church. God is writing my story. When we write our own story, chances are we end up writing from some of our own hurt, pain, and bad experiences.

When you allow God to write your story he can take all of our kairos moments (the good, the bad, the ugly, and the beautiful) and turn them into an unbelievable best seller. So when Jesus looked out into this field, he saw some New York Times best selling autobiographies. He saw an incredible harvest.

LOVE LESSON:

The harvest is local, regional, and global (Acts 1:8).

LOVE QUESTION:

What is the spiritual condition of your city? What does the harvest look like?

LOVE APPLICATION:

How can you apply this devotional to your life?

LOVE NOTES:

What stuck out to you?

What else is God saying to you?

DAY

OUR DISRUPTION

"Your love for one another will prove to the world that you are my disciples." — John 13:35 NLT

"Dreadlocks, fades and fitteds / A multi-cultural faith community that's committed / To the great commandment and the great commission / We orthodox in our beliefs – but not in our fishing"

"UN.ORTHODOX" - URBAN D. (UN.ORTHODOX ALBUM)

There are many churches that are declining, dwindling, and dying as they refuse to make necessary changes as culture and demographics around them rapidly shift. But, in the midst of the bad news, there are several bright spots where churches are thriving as they engage their changing communities. They are reaching the harvest and seeing true church growth and revitalization as they learn to create new paths of ministry.

These are some amazing stories from some friends who have learned to adapt to the disruption. As we learn to love our cities in new ways, this could become our finest hour!

Ken Claytor – *Founder and Lead Pastor – Alive Church*

The goal was simple. To have a church that resembles heaven. Or so I thought. I remember living outside of Washington, DC when God first called us to Gainesville, Florida. I didn't know much about Gainesville. In fact, I had to Google it to figure out where it was after the Lord spoke it. However, the one thing I did know for sure was that we were going to build a multi-racial church. But I didn't know how challenging that would be to accomplish as a young black man. I remember at the beginning of our ministry. There was a lady who asked my wife so gently, "is it ok, If I come to your church?" She said, "of course, we would love for you to come." Completely naïve at the moment, we had no idea that she was concerned about coming because she was…white.

It has always amazed me that whites and blacks and everyone in between can work together in corporate America Monday through Friday, pass the football together all day on Saturday, but Sunday morning is the most segregated time of our week. We had to do something about this. We wanted our church to resemble heaven. At the time, we were 98% black in attendance, but our city was 23% black. We tried it all. We said we were a church for "all people". We invited white guest speakers. We photo-shopped pictures to market our church as being diverse. It worked to get them in the door. But, unfortunately, most wouldn't stay.

What did we do? I am glad you asked. Ultimately, it is the favor and grace of God. There were several things combined that we did that caused this change, but the major one was that we decided to be very intentional. We decided that our church would resemble heaven no matter what the costs. That means that we became intentional about who is on stage, who is on our website, who is on our videos, and who is at first impression points of our church. We needed

to make sure that new guests felt like "They belonged". Our music reflects that intentionality. We had to make sure that our music wasn't to black or too white. We had to find an in-between that all could enjoy. Our staff reflects that. We could not have a staff that was off pace with the demographics of our city. If we are going to win our city, we need our staff and leadership to reflect the demographics of our city. Some might say that that seems fleshy. The truth is the exact opposite in our eyes. We naturally go to people who look like us, talk like us, and have our same characteristics. However, there is power in diversity. We learn so much more and grow so much more when we get out of our bubble. However, diversity does not happen by accident. It doesn't matter how much we pray. It only happens when we take God's love, and we become intentional about who we want to reach and go out of our way to make them feel like they belong.

As a black pastor, I didn't have many models to learn from. This was years of trial and error. I saw a lot of white pastors with multi cultural churches, but not a lot of black leaders. Our call and our assignment was to have a church that looks like heaven and reflects our city. John 13:35 states, "By this everyone will know that you are my disciples, if you love one another". Alive Church has grown to have locations in Gainesville, Orlando, and Tampa. Thousands of people are part of this diverse church that is growing and reaching new people for Jesus every week. Racism is not just a natural problem. It is a spiritual problem. The devil would love for us to stay divided. A kingdom divided against itself can never stand. My prayer is that the world will begin to look to the church for answers on racial reconciliation. Racism has never been a skin issue. It has always been a sin issue. God's love is the key.

David Crosby, D.Min

Founder and Lead Pastor - Community Church

My wife, Bekah, and I planted Community Church over twenty years ago in the heart of the beautiful Pocono Mountains, Pennsylvania. Historically known as a resort community, the Poconos has more recently become a bedroom community to northern New Jersey and New York since it is located only 68 miles from Manhattan. Over thirty thousand people commute an hour and a half one way from the Poconos into New York City and New Jersey every day. The Poconos became the fastest growing community in Pennsylvania for over 10 years in the late 1980s and 1990s, with thousands of "transplants" moving from the city into the

9

mountains. We had another surge of new people leaving the city and coming to our community during the pandemic. This has created a new community geographic definition known as post-rural – a rural community comprised of both rural and city people.

Of course, this reality has had a great impact on the culture of Community Church. I describe Community Church this way: if the hit television show "Duck Dynasty" got together with the hit show, "The Housewives of New Jersey" – and they had a baby – that would be our church. It's a beautiful collection of both rednecks and city slickers. Take one look at our lobby, and you will see a lot of stilettoes and camouflage walking around. In fact, we now have over 40 nations represented in our church without one dominant ethnic culture. It's a beautiful living picture of what heaven will look like one day, with every tongue and tribe on earth worshiping together in community.

When starting Community Church, we honestly had no specific intention of planting a multicultural church. We simply had an abiding love for people and the desire to build a "whosoever" church. The Bible says, "For whosoever shall call upon the name of the Lord shall be saved." (Romans 10:13 KJV) However, we quickly began to realize that our church was ethnically diverse, with three predominant people groups: African Americans, Whites, and Hispanics. One weekend, about a year or so into the church plant, it occurred to me as I stood stage of the high school auditorium where our portable church got its start that I was the only white person standing on the stage. I found myself surrounded by a Jamaican, a Trinidadian, a Guyanese, a Puerto Rican, and an Italian man from Brooklyn, but Brooklyn counts as its own country in my book. If you ever had the pleasure of knowing someone from Brooklyn you would agree.

Leading a multicultural congregation is the future of the church in America. It's been my long-held belief that your congregation should be a mirror reflection of the community in which it's located. So if you live in a diverse community, you should worship in a diverse church. Racial reconciliation and social justice are central to the Gospel. Jesus himself stood for inclusivity over exclusivity. We see this when he entered the temple where the money changers had set up shop in the outer Gentile court. Jesus famously turned over the tables and threw out the money changers, not just because they were exploiting the poor but because they had pushed out an entire people group from worshipping in the presence of God - the Gentiles. That's why he said in that moment, " Is it not written: 'My house will be called a house of prayer for all nations'? (Mark 11:17) Jesus' house is for all nations. If Jesus were a Puerto Rican, he would've said it this way, "Mi casa es su casa." My house is your house.

LOVE LESSON:

Although many churches are declining and dying, there are also several that are growing and thriving as they learn to adapt to the changes in their communities.

LOVE QUESTION:

What story resonated with you and why?

LOVE APPLICATION:

How can you apply this devotional to your life?

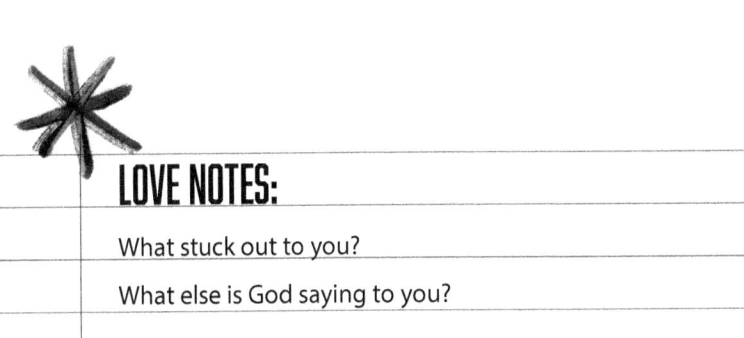

LOVE NOTES:

What stuck out to you?

What else is God saying to you?

LOVE
our City

DAY 10

OUR NEIGHBOR

"The man answered, 'You must love the Lord your God with all your heart, all your soul and all your strength, and all your mind.' And, 'Love your neighbor as you love yourself.'" — Luke 10:27 NLT

"He revised this Samaritan's title to Good / Because he stopped and helped this beat up Jew like a true neighbor would / Even though their people had beef / And if that Jew wasn't hurt he might have actually given that Samaritan some grief.

"WILL YOU BE MY NEIGHBOR?" - URBAN D. (LOVE OUR CITY ALBUM)

There was a religious leader who stepped up to Jesus and tried to antagonize him and justify himself at the same time. This guy knew the Mosaic Law inside and out. He asked Jesus, "Teacher, what should I do to inherit eternal life?" Jesus replied in classic form and answered with a question. Actually, two questions! He said, "What does the law of Moses say? How do you read it?" The religious leader answered, "You must love the Lord your God with all your heart, all your soul, all your strength, and all your mind. And love your neighbor as you love yourself." Jesus agreed and told him, "Right, do this, and you will live." So that part of the conversation went well, but here is where it gets interesting. Luke 10:29 tells us, "The man wanted to justify his actions, so he asked Jesus, 'And who is my neighbor?'"

This religious leader was basically trying to choose who he would love, and who he could cross off his neighbor list. He was looking for a loophole. He wanted to just love people who looked like him, were from the same income bracket, and lived in the same neighborhood. You know... the same tribe. Unfortunately, a lot of people still operate like this. A lot of Christians and a lot of churches operate like this. Many of them may not even do it with full intentionality. It just comes naturally. It's more comfortable to be around people like you. In chapter one, we talked about our comfort problem.

But, if you look at this word neighbor, there isn't a loophole. It literally means your neighbors: those who you live around, work around, play around, shop around... aka your city! In the Greek language, it means "Someone who is near." The people near us in our cities are not just one ethnic group, one age demographic, one class, or one culture - they are diverse. So when my diverse church does Love Our City outreach events, we always have people asking us, "Why are you doing this?" Their surprised expressions are funny, but sad. They can't believe this diverse group of people is giving something away and showing love with no strings attached. Who does that? Apparently, almost no one nowadays! The media have shown up at our events and asked us the same question, "Why are you doing this?" Our response is that we take the words of Jesus seriously. He told us to love our neighbors as we love ourselves. We are putting that into action. We care about our neighbors, and we are striving to make our city a better place. They are blown away.

So, back to the story in Luke 10. What did Jesus say to this guy who was looking for a loophole? Jesus replied with a story about a priest, a religious guy, and a Samaritan. It almost sounds like the beginning of a joke, right? But it was no joke! In verse 30, Jesus said, "A Jewish man was traveling from Jerusalem down to Jericho, and he was attacked by bandits. They stripped him of his clothes, beat him up, and left him half dead beside the road. By chance, a priest came

along, but when he saw the man lying there, he crossed to the other side of the road and passed by." What? The priest just passed him by? If anyone had helped him, I would have thought it would be the priest. He's a pastor. A shepherd. A spiritual leader. Maybe he was in a hurry? It was a seventeen-mile journey between Jerusalem and Jericho, and maybe it was about to get dark. He also may have been worried that it was a trap, that if he stopped and helped the guy, he might have been jumped too. I don't know. I'm trying to give him the benefit of the doubt, but it still seems a little messed up.

Jesus continued the story and said, "A temple assistant walked over and looked at him lying there, but he also passed on the other side of the road." So this second religious man stopped and looked at him, but he decided to keep going as well. Wow, we're zero for two, and they were both leaders from the church. Not a good look! But now, here is where it gets interesting. This third guy comes rolling up in verse 33. Jesus said, "Then a despised Samaritan came along, and when he saw the man, he had compassion on him." Did you catch that? What kind of Samaritan? Despised. But wait, most of us probably heard about the Samaritan before, and it wasn't the story of the despised Samaritan... it was the Good Samaritan! What's up with that? If you don't know the historical context, you can miss the punchline.

Jesus highlights this Samaritan as the good guy, but in their culture, the Samaritans were known as the bad guys. There was no such thing as a Good Samaritan. You had these two religious dudes walk right by the half-dead man on the side of the road, but you have this Samaritan come up and have real compassion. The man who was hurt was Jewish. Samaritans were considered a totally different ethnic group as they were only partly Jewish. They intermarried with foreigners and adopted some of their idolatrous customs. They were considered half-breeds and universally despised by Jews. In addition to that, the Samaritans built their own temple on Mount Gerizam which they insisted was designated by Moses as the true place of worship for the nation. Samaria was also a place of refuge for Jewish people who were criminals running from the Jewish authorities. If Jews were traveling from Jerusalem to Judea, the shortest way was to go directly north and pass through Samaria to get there. But, they were known to go east and cross the Jordan River and then go north and bypass Samaria, then go west and cross the Jordan river again to get to Judea. This added an additional twenty-five miles to their trip. They didn't want to pass through Samaritan towns, drink from their wells, or have any contact with them. As you can see, there was a lot of drama between the Samaritans and the Jews.

The Samaritans were outsiders. They were misfits. They were considered to be second-class citizens. But, Jesus shares

this story of the Samaritan looking at this hurt Jew as his neighbor. He was a human who was made in the image of God. Even though this hurt Jew probably hated Samaritans and would have despised him and judged him if he were well. The Samaritan still showed him love. Look at what happened next. "Going over to him, the Samaritan soothed his wounds with olive oil and wine and bandaged them. Then he put the man on his own donkey and took him to an inn, where he took care of him. The next day, he handed the innkeeper two silver coins, telling him, 'Take care of this man. If his bill runs higher than this, I'll pay you the next time I'm here.' Then Jesus asked him, 'Now which of these three would you say was a neighbor to the man that was attacked by bandits?' The man replied, 'The one who showed him mercy.' Then Jesus said, 'Yes, now go and do the same.'"

The Samaritan was the surprise hero of this story. It wasn't the priest or the Levite, it was the despised half-breed. Jesus is drawing a strong contrast between those who knew the law and those who actually followed the law in their lifestyle and actions. Jesus gives this example of someone unexpected being a good neighbor and says, now you go and do the same. There's no loophole. If a Samaritan can love someone who literally hates him, then you can too! If we're honest, many of us can relate to that religious leader who asked Jesus 'Who is my neighbor?' There are times when we don't feel like getting out of our comfort zone. We would rather hang around people who are more like us. We would rather show love to people that we know will show love back to us. But God puts people in our paths for a reason. It may be a homeless person who smells and is mentally unstable. It may be someone of a different skin color or age. It may be someone who is Muslim wearing a Hijab. When we see these differences, it can sometimes cause us to look the other way or think that we can't reach them. Many times, we are the exact person that God wants to use in that moment.

LOVE LESSON:

There is no loophole in what Jesus said, "Love your neighbors. Our neighbors are literally "Those that are near"; those we live around, work around, play around, shop around (our city).

LOVE QUESTION:

Why did Jesus use a "Despised" Samaritan as the surprise hero of the story in Luke 10?

LOVE APPLICATION:

How can you apply this devotional to your life?

LOVE NOTES:

What stuck out to you?

What else is God saying to you?

LOVE Our City

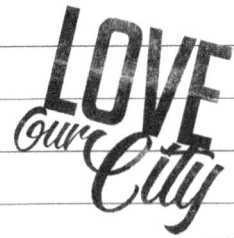

DAY

11

OUR THIRST

"Jesus replied, 'Anyone who drinks this water will soon become thirsty again. But those who drink the water I give will never be thirsty again. It becomes a fresh, bubbling spring within them, giving them eternal life.'" — John 4:13-14 NLT

"The American Dream / It's not all that it seems / From the ghetto to Wall Street – it's money making schemes / From suits and ties – to Tims and Jeans / Most just need to be redeemed"

"THE AMERICAN DREAM" – URBAN D. FEAT. COREY RED & PRECISE (THE IMMIGRANT ALBUM)

11

e don't love our neighbor to earn God's love. We love our neighbor as an expression of what God has already done for us. God loved us first, even when we were in the middle of our dirt. He loved us when we didn't deserve it. He loved us when we didn't expect it. He pursued us. Now, we get the opportunity to do this for others. We reach out to people in the middle of their junk, even if they don't deserve it. They may be ungrateful and be in the middle of a mess that they created. They might have a bad attitude and get nasty with us. But don't catch amnesia. Many of us were like this during a season of our lives, and God used someone to pursue us and show us love, right when we needed it. Let's pursue our neighbors and love them with no strings attached. The Samaritan loved this beat-up Jew on the side of the road. He was a hot mess. He may not have even been grateful as a despised Samaritan was helping him. The Samaritan still loved him, cleaned him up, and paid for his hotel room with no strings attached. This not only impacted that hurt man, but it is still impacting us today as we read about it and ponder the application to our lives.

With God's help, we must learn to shift our attitude towards our neighbors, especially the ones who give us attitude. There are three attitudes displayed in this story that Jesus told in Luke 10. The Robbers' attitude was "What's yours is mine, and I'm going to take it." The Priest and the Levite's attitude was "What's mine is mine and I'm going to keep it." The Samaritan's attitude was "What's mine is yours, and I'm going to share it." Which attitude is yours today? Dr. Martin Luther King Jr. preached from this story in Luke the night before he was killed. The sermon was called "I've been to the mountaintop." Dr. King pointed out that the priest and the Levite didn't stop to help the man because, in essence, they asked themselves the question, "If I stop to help, what will happen to me?" But the Samaritan asked a much different question: "If I don't stop, what will happen to him?" Are we really concerned about what happens to our neighbors?

We live in a world where everyone is thirsty. They are looking for happiness, peace, contentment, purpose, and pleasure. They are trying to find it in all kinds of ways. I had a season of my life where I tried to quench my thirst with material things, girls, and popularity, but at the end of the day, I was left even more thirsty. I was drinking from the wrong well. Many of our neighbors are drinking from the wrong well with poisonous water. And poison makes us sick... and sick people do what? They make other people sick, just like hurt people - hurt people. Broken people - break people. But, on the flip side, forgiven people - forgive people, healed people - heal people, and loved people - love people. So, there is hope and healing available, even if you've gone through some deep issues. Hurt and abuse are complex subjects. There can be lots of layers: sexually, verbally, physically, and emotionally. With all the people reading this, I realize there are many holding this book in their hands that have been abused. As a pastor and spiritual leader, I want to say I'm so sorry for what you've gone through. I acknowledge your hurt and pain. I want to let you know that you matter! It makes me angry that you had to go through that; that is why I felt this needed to be included in a book about loving other people. Some of us still have some big holes and big wounds. It's hard to love when you leak. Even if you haven't gone through hurt personally, you know someone who has. God wants to use this book to equip all of us to help restore people as we follow the example of Jesus.

In the gospel of John, Chapter 4, we see another story about an unlikely neighbor. Jesus met a Samaritan Woman at a well. This happened because Jesus chose to travel through Samaria with his disciples. Instead of going the normal Jewish bypass route that was twenty-five miles out of the way, he took the less-preferred route directly through Samaria. Jesus asked this woman for a drink of water. She was shocked and expressed it to him, as men normally didn't speak to women in public. Even greater than that, he was a Jew and she was a Samaritan. Jesus replied, "If you only knew the gift God has for you and who you are speaking to, you would ask me, and I would give you living water." She still didn't understand, as she stated that Jesus didn't have a bucket and that she didn't think he could offer better water than Jacob's well had. Jesus then told her, "Anyone who drinks this water will soon become thirsty again. But those who drink the water I give will never be thirsty again. It becomes a fresh, bubbling spring within them, giving them eternal life." This Samaritan woman was thirsty, and this caught her attention. She asked Jesus to please give her some of this incredible-sounding water; she was tired of having to come to get water at this well. That's when Jesus asked her to go and get her husband. She told him that she didn't have a husband. Then Jesus read her email and told her that she previously had five different husbands, and she was currently living with a man that she wasn't married to. She admitted he was right.

This woman had a tough life. There may have been abuse, sexual, verbal, or physical. She was done with marriage, as the man she was with now was not her husband. She was thirsty. She had been through a lot of pain and a lot of loss. But that day, she discovered the living water and went back to her village and shared with everyone about this encounter. All of us have experienced some drought seasons, which can leave us dry. But there is living water that can eternally quench our thirst. Jesus makes it available to us so we can share it with our neighbors.

LOVE LESSON:

We don't love our neighbor to earn God's love. We love our neighbor as an expression of what God has already done for us.

LOVE QUESTION:

We are all thirsty. What well (what you watch and listen to) are you regularly drinking from?

LOVE APPLICATION:

How can you apply this devotional to your life?

LOVE NOTES:

What stuck out to you?

What else is God saying to you?

LOVE our City

DAY
12

OUR A.I.

"If you need wisdom, ask our generous God, and he will give it to you. He will not rebuke you for asking."
— James 1:5 NLT

This times are pivotable / The masses are captured by the digital / Sucked in by the eye candy, the message is usually subliminal / Never minimal / The way they pimp the propaganda is criminal.

"THE BIG SCREEN" - URBAN D. (UN.HEARD ALBUM)

*E*very morning before your first cup of coffee, AI has already shaped your neighbors. Your neighbor across the street asked ChatGPT to write a challenging email for a situation at his job. The teenager who works at the grocery store woke up to an algorithm-curated social media feed. The lady who walks her dog past your house every day applied for a new job, and an unseen hiring algorithm filtered her resume before any human even saw it. Your depressed next-door neighbor asked Gemini private questions they are afraid to ask anyone else. Our neighbors all around us are being shaped by AI's imprint. And it's not just our neighbors, it's us. Even if you are not intentionally using AI, it is integrated into more systems than you realize.

AI can be used as a great tool to help automate systems, take away mundane tasks, and quickly give us the information we are looking for. There are many benefits, but also some dangers. Students can use it to cheat. Criminals can use it to scam and steal. Everyday people can get lazier and use it to do our thinking. A study revealed that using ChatGPT over time actually shrinks the brain [1]. When you continually rely on it to do your thinking, if it is then taken away, your brain cannot easily do certain tasks, as over time your neural pathways were rewired and have less function.

All of us have algorithms running on nearly every screen we look at. These AI-created algorithms curate our Netflix,

Spotify, and Social Media feeds. It basically feeds us more of what it thinks we would like, so we'll stay on the platforms longer and have a more enjoyable experience. Sounds good, right? Well, not so fast. What can happen is we get stuck seeing the same type of news, posts, ads, and information. You can find yourself in an echo chamber where everything is in the same line of thinking. Many people have an entirely different online experience compared to their neighbors. You can fool yourself into thinking you have the right perspective and everyone thinks just like you… And you might be thinking that way because you have only been presented one side of the information. This is called confirmation bias. One of the dangers of AI is that the algorithm seems to be pushing people to the extremes of the right and the left, and the middle has been disappearing.

I believe our job as believers in Jesus is to pull people to a healthy middle where we have a balance. I intentionally look at Fox News, CNN, BBC, and more. They all lean differently, and they report news from a different slant. I follow some people on social media that I don't fully agree with, so I can see how they are thinking and what they are talking about. If you want to truly love your neighbors and reach them for Jesus, you have to be aware of some of what their algorithm is feeding them. I'm not saying we subject ourselves to profanity or X-rated material, but we can still be aware of what is happening in the world around us and some of the things

that might be trending in culture. Paul said in 1 Corinthians 9:22, "I become all things to all people so that by all possible means I might save some." We take all of this information and filter it through the discernment of the Holy Spirit and how he would have us move.

As AI develops more and more, there are people turning to it for advice, therapy, counseling, and even friendship. This is where we can start to cross some lines. Instead of building healthy relationships with friends, family, and neighbors, we can isolate ourselves from humans as we rely more and more on an AI program. The theologian Augustine wrote that curiosity can lead us either toward wisdom or away from it. He called the first studiositas, which is a curiosity born of love and a desire to better understand, so we can serve better. That fits right in with this book. The other he called curiosities, which is a restless hunger to know for its own sake, to master what should instead invite reverence. If you think about it, AI tests which path we will choose. It tempts us with speed and wonder. Wow... we can ask it whatever, and in just seconds it spits out an answer right before our eyes. But, we must be careful because at times it is an illusion of wisdom without real-life encounters. Real wisdom is usually not quick. It takes time and grows in relationship and experience. It learns through listening and humbles itself when faced with mystery.

AI is not our enemy. It can be somewhat of a mirror. It can reflect the kind of person we are and the person we are becoming. If we use it selfishly, it can grow our pride, isolation, and impatience. But, if we use it to grow our compassion, to notice our neighbors that the world forgets, it might help us become more like Jesus. It can literally free up some of our time so we can be more present with loving our city. It can open up new doors for learning, connection, and care that once weren't possible due to distance or time. But, it can't replace our human love. Every advance in AI and tech can't replace the two most important commandments - to love God and neighbor with our full attention.

LOVE LESSON:

Artificial Intelligence cannot replace our creator, and it can't replace human love.

LOVE QUESTION:

How are you using AI? Is it in a healthy way?

LOVE APPLICATION:

How can you apply this devotional to your life?

LOVE NOTES:

What stuck out to you?

What else is God saying to you?

DAY

13

OUR R.O.I.

"Look, I am coming soon, bringing my reward with me to repay all people according to their deeds."
— Revelation 22:12 NLT

"Because you can't take nothing when you leave this planet / It's all about faith - that's the way that he planned it / I'll stay true, keep rockin' microphones and flowing / Cuz I know up above my inheritance is growing"

"ENDURANCE" - URBAN D. (THE MISSIN' ELEMENT ALBUM)

13

We are great at wasting things. If you live in America, you are some of the biggest wasters in the world. We lead the world in food waste as we throw away 150,000 tons of food every day [1]. We only make up 5% of the world's population, but we use 24% of the world's energy [2]. Many of us waste our resources, our time, our talent, and even our lives! Loving our neighbor is never a waste of time, talent, or resources. Jesus told us that even if we give a cup of cold water in his name, we will be rewarded. He will remember our labor of love. The scripture tells us to store up our treasures in heaven. Everything here is temporary, as the average person lives less than eighty years, but in a million years from now, we'll still be in heaven. Yet, most of us are only focused on storing up treasures here for mere decades. We're investing in the things we think will bring us the biggest ROI (Return on Investment) while we're here. As I'm writing this, the stock market is breaking new records, real estate prices have risen, and cryptocurrency continues to create new millionaires.

People are dreaming about how they can make the right investment moves that could change their lives. I'll admit, it can be easy to get caught up in this, as I've watched some people I know make a lot of money in investments. But I've also watched some people lose a lot in high-risk investments. Either way, in the big picture, it is all just temporary. If I could pay off my house, that would be great, but in one hundred years from now, it won't matter much. I won't be here, and my house might not even be standing.

The things that are really going to have the greatest ROI are eternal investments. We can't take any of our stuff with us. In the future, someone else will be living in my house, and my cars, clothes, and technology will all be obsolete. The only things we can really take into eternity are people. If we invest in our neighbor's lives and they start a relationship with Christ, then we will see them again in eternity. The Bible talks about rewards in heaven. The concept of this is illustrated in the New Testament teaching by the use of the Greek word in Matthew 16:27 that is translated as "reward". This word literally means a paycheck. This eternal compensation that we are to receive is not some free gift, but it's an actual payback for the work that was done for God. Revelation 22:12 says something very similar where Jesus says, "I am coming soon, bringing my reward with me to repay all people according to their deeds." I like the way the Message Translation says it, "Yes, I'm on the way! I'll be there soon! I'm bringing my payroll with me. I'll pay all people in full for their life's work."

So all of us have an account in heaven where our permanent net worth is being increased by our life's work for God; our deeds, our giving, our love. Whatever we accumulate here is just temporary net worth, but we increase our permanent net worth when we follow the words of Jesus

and we love our neighbor. Jesus shares that he is preparing an amazing place for us. We can dream and imagine that it is going to be incredible, but there is some mystery to it, as I think there should be. What if we could see what we were going to get? Did you ever think about that? What if we could go to heaven.com and type in our user name and password, and we could see how our treasures in heaven were looking?

What if we could watch our permanent, eternal net worth rise? Picture this with me... That day, you might bring your neighbor to church, pray for someone at work, and feed some homeless people on the way home... only to see how your investment grew. So you log into heaven.com, and you can see that your house went from a 3 bedroom to a 5 bedroom. You see where I'm going with this? What would we do then? We would go out and love our neighbors more than ever, so we could see our investment increasing. For many of us, it would probably become addictive in a not so good way. Our motives could become selfish and self-centered, and we would miss the things God wants to genuinely do in us and through us. So, keep in mind there are incredible rewards in store for us when we serve God's purposes here on earth, but stay focused on the task at hand.

Jesus wants his church to find ways to build bridges with our neighbors and show them the love of Christ in real and tangible ways. He wants us to love people who are different than us. They may not actually live in our neighborhoods, but they work there or shop there. They are present in our city. We need to find ways to engage them and demonstrate unconditional love. So here is our application for this chapter: we can all be better neighbors! Biblical love transcends boundaries of geography, race, religion, socio-economic status, and even convenience. Loving our city is not just a project, an event, or even a week of serving. It should become a lifestyle. Imagine someday in heaven where people come up to you and thank you for changing their eternity. Some of them you know and have spent time discipling, while others you never even met. They might have been impacted through your service or some content you posted or created. So don't waste all your time chasing after temporary investments; think about the ones that will last forever.

LOVE LESSON:

Our earthly net worth is temporary, but our heavenly net worth is permanent.

LOVE QUESTION:

What are some things that you can do to increase your heavenly net worth and cause you to "store up treasures in heaven?"

LOVE APPLICATION:

How can you apply this devotional to your life?

LOVE NOTES:

What stuck out to you?

What else is God saying to you?

DAY 14

OURSELVES

"And you must love the Lord your God with all your heart, all your soul, all your mind, and all your strength. The second is equally important: 'Love your neighbor as yourself.' No other commandment is greater than these." — Mark 12:30-31 NLT

"Me versus you, my people versus yours / Division, Division, Division, Divorce / It's tearing our cities apart at the core / You have to know we're created for more!

"LOVE OUR CITY 2.0" - URBAN D. FEAT. SPECHOUSE, LONGBOI & DEYANA
(LOVE OUR CITY ALBUM)

esus told us the second most important commandment is to "Love our neighbor as we love ourselves." Some of us may think the problem isn't learning to love our neighbor, but it is learning to love ourselves. A lot of us have issues with ourselves. We can think before we can "Love our city, our neighbors, our spouses, our kids, and our friends… we need to first learn to love ourselves. Some of us might initially interpret it like this. I've read into it this way myself. But that's not what Jesus is speaking of in these verses.

Jesus is saying that we start with this human trait of loving ourselves. All of us have a powerful instinct of self-preservation and self-fulfillment. We want to be happy and satisfied. We strive for it. We fight for it. We want food for ourselves, things for ourselves, a place to live for ourselves. We want our lives to be significant. We want to matter. All of that is self-love. You could boil it down to a deep longing to diminish pain and to increase happiness. This is a human trait that is hardwired into all of us. It causes us to move forward and function each day. It is not a bad thing, but it is not always manifested in a healthy way.

Even in our selfishness, we are still fighting for ourselves. Even if we are in survival mode or in a really unhealthy place, at the root, we are trying to protect ourselves. So Jesus is talking about this thing inside of us that we don't have to learn. It's already built in us. To hunger for food is not evil. To want to be warm in the winter is not evil. To want to be healthy is not evil. So this human trait is not evil in itself. If it has become evil in your life, that will become evident in how you respond to Jesus' command of "love your neighbor as you love yourself. So just like you feed yourself when you get hungry, will you feed your hungry neighbor when they need it? Just like you work to live in a comfortable place, do you desire that for your neighbor? As you seek to be safe from violence, do you seek security for your neighbor? As you look for friends yourself, are you being a friend to your neighbor? As you are striving to advance in your career, will you help your neighbor advance in theirs? In other words, make your self-seeking equal to your self-giving.

The big word in the command "Love your neighbor as you love yourself" is not just "love". Everyone's thoughts immediately move to the word "love". But the challenging word here is "as". So if you are innovative and entrepreneurial in pursuing your own happiness and building your dream, be just as innovative for your neighbor's dream. If you are passionate and over the top about your family, be just as passionate that your neighbor will have a healthy family. Wow. If we really take Jesus at his word here, that is pretty intense. "As ourselves" is pretty deep as we love us some us. It can seem overwhelming and not humanly possible. That is why it is important to take this statement in full context. We

need the first commandment to be able to fulfill the second commandment. Remember, the first commandment is "Love the Lord your God with all your heart and with all your soul and with all your mind." The first commandment is the basis for the second one. The second commandment is the visible expression of the first commandment. Before you are self-seeking or self-giving of love, you have to first put God in that number one spot of receiving your love.

When we truly learn to apply the first commandment to our lives, we will find true satisfaction and love. Our self-love, solely focused on ourselves, will leave us empty and confused. God says, come to me, and I will give you fullness of joy. Our lives are then transformed, and we have this joy that is spilling out of us. This is when we start loving ourselves in a healthy and balanced way. I could have spent a lot of time in this short chapter giving information about how to learn to love ourselves better. But, we all know there are a lot of people who love themselves in a very narcissistic way. There are already tons of self-help books and materials out there. But, to keep it simple, if you put God first and love him with all your heart, soul, and mind, then you will have a healthy heart, soul, and mind. You'll love yourself properly, and that will put you in a position to live out the second command. It comes more naturally as we now have proper self-love that can be the source of our neighbor-love.

Remember that Jesus gave himself for the world. He gave his life for us even though we didn't deserve it or earn it. Even though we were still unclean sinners, he died for us because he loved us so much. Jesus is sharing these commands with a Jewish audience. The Jews were God's chosen people, and some of them felt like they had the market cornered on God's affection. They felt like they were superior. Jesus was also saying to love the neighbor that you think is unclean. Love them like they are clean. We may not walk around thinking we are superior, but there may be some people around us that we would consider unclean. I'm not just talking about someone who is physically dirty. It may be that person with the vulgar mouth at work or school. It may be a friend who is always negative and complaining. It may be your crazy uncle who always says inappropriate things. Every family has a crazy uncle. Whether we think it consciously or subconsciously, there are people around us we may consider unclean. We exclude them from the list of people that we could love as much as we love ourselves. I know, it's hard. This is where the transforming power of Christ works on our hearts. This is a process when we upgrade our everyday lenses so we can see all people through the eyes of Christ.

LOVE LESSON:

The second commandment is the visible expression of following the first commandment.

LOVE QUESTION:

Is there anyone I struggle with loving "as" much as I would love myself? Why? How can I work on this?

LOVE APPLICATION:

How can you apply this devotional to your life?

14

LOVE NOTES:

What stuck out to you?

What else is God saying to you?

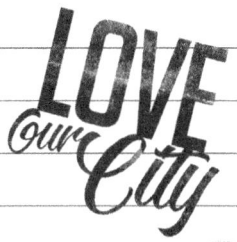

LOVE our City

WEEK 2 VIDEO SERIES

PLAY VIDEO

1. We are called to _____ our neighbor, but many times our neighbor can end up being a _____ to us.

2. Many people _____ the truth and even _____ the truth, but don't always _____ the truth.

"Then a despised Samaritan came along, and when he saw the man, he felt compassion for him. Going over to him, the Samaritan soothed his wounds with olive oil and wine and bandaged them. Then he put the man on his own donkey and took him to an inn, where he took care of him." — Luke 10:33-34 NLT.

3. Jesus switched the image of the Samaritan from _____ to _____. He flipped the script and made the Samaritan the hero of the story.

4. Jesus was _____ racism and discrimination.

5. The Gospel is not exclusive it's _____.

6. Paul's model was he reached people that became his spiritual sons, that transitioned into becoming his students and then eventually they became his _____ in ministry.

DISCUSSION QUESTIONS

1. Have you ever blessed someone in some way, and it ended up being more of a blessing for you than it did for them? What happened?

Read Luke 10:25-37

2. Have you ever been in such a hurry that you missed an opportunity to help a neighbor?

3. Have you ever judged someone and had a bad impression of them, but once you got to know them, they were a great person?

4. Have you experienced racism or discrimination?

5. Who is the person or people who were instrumental in helping you grow in your relationship with Christ?

6. Do you have anyone in your life that would fit in that role of a spiritual son or daughter, a student, or a partner? If not… who could that be?

DAY 15

OUR LEADER

"But among you it will be different. Whoever wants to be a leader among you must be your servant."
— Matthew 20:26 NLT

"Whether you're young or you're old, single or married / The way that you Display (serve) might be varied / At home, or at work, even at church / Come on family – we gotta put in work!"

"LIFE IN 3D" - URBAN D. FEAT. ANTHONY VALOR (AMNESIA EP)

We live in a culture that is generally self-serving. The higher you climb up the corporate ladder, the more perks you have and the more people are there to serve you and take care of your needs. We see celebrities walk around with their entourage that handles every little detail of their lives. This has been the model for thousands of years. Many people think this is the definition of success.

But Jesus set a new example as he turned this idea upside down. In the gospels, there were several times when the disciples argued about who was the greatest. They wanted the perks and the attention. Jesus regularly put them in their place and let them know that is not the way we roll. Then he said something that was extremely counter-cultural, "Whoever wants to be a leader among you must be your servant."

Jesus didn't just say it, but there were actions to back it up. Throughout his ministry, he served people and sacrificed many conveniences of everyday life. He was basically couch surfing, staying at different people's homes as they traveled from city to city. Jesus poured out and had many long days of teaching, traveling, and meeting people's needs. He was constantly giving himself. His disciples saw this firsthand as they were right there with him. For some reason, it still didn't click for most of them at first. But one of the things that personally impacted them in a huge way was when he washed their feet. Washing someone's feet in Jewish culture was for someone at the very bottom of the ladder.

The disciples regularly argued with each other about who was the greatest. They didn't want to wash each other's feet, as whoever did it first would then be admitting they weren't the greatest. But their leader - the miracle worker, healer, and famous teacher took his robe off, tied it around his waste and bent down to wash their nasty feet. He set the example. It was a groundbreaking moment. Loud-mouthed Peter protested and told Jesus he would never let Him wash his feet. He didn't think it was proper as Jesus was his master. But Jesus told him if He didn't, he wouldn't belong to him. Peter quickly obliged.

After Jesus washed His disciples' feet, He put his robe back on and said this in John 13:12-15, "Do you understand what I was doing? You call me 'Teacher' and 'Lord,' and you are right, because that's what I am. And since I, your Lord and Teacher, have washed your feet, you ought to wash each other's feet. I have given you an example to follow. Do as I have done to you." If our leader and savior can bend down and wash feet, then we must be ready to roll up our sleeves and get dirty as well.

Throughout the gospels, we can see how Jesus set the tone of reaching out to the lost, the forgotten, and the unwanted: the woman at the well, tax collectors, lepers, the demon-possessed, prostitutes, and even dirty fishermen. He told stories that made despised Samaritans the heroes and went places that most religious leaders of his day would never step foot in. If Jesus were here today, he would be reaching out to all kinds of lost people in our communities: the corrupt businessmen, the strippers, the drug dealers, the gang members, the atheist college students, the prescription drug addicts, and even the Muslim woman wearing a hijab. Jesus set the pace, and we need to follow his lead.

LOVE LESSON:

If you want to be a real leader, you must become a real servant.

LOVE QUESTION:

What is a recent way you have served someone?

LOVE APPLICATION:

How can you apply this devotional to your life?

LOVE NOTES:

What stuck out to you?

What else is God saying to you?

LOVE
Our City

DAY 16

OUR EXAMPLE

"I tell you, her sins – and they are many – have been forgiven, so she has shown me much love. But a person who is forgiven little shows only little love." — Luke 7:47 NLT

"Cristos Si agapo Puli, / Read the holy scriptures - learn about they family tree / Check the bloodline from Moses, to David, to Nehemiah, Paul, Joseph, John, Thomas, Jeremiah / We all from one seed / Red's the color we all bleed / Take heed / Watering your spiritual roots is what you need.

"ROOTS" - URBAN D. FEAT. CRUZ CORDERO (UN.HEARD ALBUM)

16

One of my favorite passages in the scripture is Luke chapter 7, where Jesus was invited to go to a religious leader's house for dinner. Now, this wasn't just any casual dinner; this was a special dinner party. Hospitality was a big deal in their culture. They had several different customs that they offered to guests. If you think about it, we also have some cultural customs in the West that we offer to special guests. When someone special comes over to my house for dinner, there are certain things I know I have to do: cut the grass, clean up the yard, vacuum, sweep and mop, and take out the trash. My daughters clean the bathrooms and straighten their rooms, and my wife works her magic in the kitchen. She'll usually cook up some Arroz con Pollo (rice and chicken), Puerto Rican style. We put away the paper plates and break out the regular plates that you actually have to wash after dinner. First-century Jewish culture took all of the things we do today to another level. They went all out. There was a VIP list for those who were invited to the dinner party. Those on the list were supposed to receive special treatment. When they arrived, they were greeted with a kiss and welcomed in a big way. A servant would remove their sandals and wash their feet. They would get them seated and offer them something to drink and eat.

When you know the cultural context of a passage of scripture, the story can become much more vivid. Luke

7:36 says, "One of the Pharisees asked Jesus to have dinner with him, so Jesus went to his home and sat down to eat." If you didn't know some of their hospitality customs, you could have missed what had just happened. On top of that, there was the context that a lot of the Pharisees didn't like Jesus. Many people in Jesus' position would not have even accepted the invitation because of the tension that already existed. We don't know exactly why Simon the Pharisee invited Jesus over to his house. Some scholars believe that some of the Pharisees were interested in His teaching or at least a bit curious. On the other hand, he may have been asking Jesus over to verbally attack Him and try to make Him look bad. We can't be sure, but what we do know is that when Jesus arrived, there were no forms of customary hospitality offered to Him.

Jesus was invited, so he was on the VIP list, but Simon, the host, ignored Him. Nobody offered to wash His feet, and no one offered Him any water to freshen up with. He was ignored as He walked in, so He went and sat down. Others saw this blatant disrespect, and it immediately began to create some tension and gossip at the party. There is another part of their culture that is very interesting and important to know when it comes to these events. These types of dinner parties usually took place in a courtyard outside of the house, and they were open to the general public. That means that anyone from the village

16

could come to the party. But the only people on the VIP list received the customary hospitality and could eat the food. But the other people could come in and stand around the edges of the party that was in the center of the courtyard. They could watch, listen, and be nosey. They didn't have wi-fi, social media, or Netflix, so the dinner parties were the place to be, even if you weren't on the VIP list.

So, you have half of the village at this dinner party, and they just saw this well-known VIP guest named Jesus get ignored as he walks in. In verse 37, it starts to get really interesting. "When a certain immoral woman from that city heard He was eating there, she brought a beautiful alabaster jar filled with expensive perfume. Then she knelt behind Him at his feet, weeping. Her tears fell on His feet, and she wiped them off with her hair. Then she kept kissing His feet and putting perfume on them."

The NLT version of scripture is being nice when it says "a certain immoral woman". Other versions describe her as the town prostitute. So imagine this courtyard full of people, some VIPs and lots of regular town people, and then this well-known prostitute walks into the party. There were all kinds of reactions. Most people were totally upset that she was there, as she was considered immoral and dirty. Some were embarrassed because they knew her, if you know what I mean. Then you had the Pharisees, who were religious leaders, and they definitely didn't want her there, as she was an unclean outsider. But she walks over to Jesus, and she pulls out this expensive bottle of Versace perfume and starts pouring it on His feet. People gasp. This is a really expensive perfume that she bought with money she earned from doing unspeakable things. How could Jesus let her do this to Him? On top of that, there was a part that most of us probably missed. She let her hair down! She was wiping Jesus' feet with it. In Middle Eastern culture, letting your hair down in public was a serious no-no. Women didn't do that. That was only for the privacy of their homes. So, to recap what just happened, Jesus is on the VIP list and walks in and gets dissed. The town prostitute walks in, pulls out this expensive perfume, takes her hair bun out, whips her hair around, and starts drying Jesus feet with it as she is uncontrollably weeping out loud and kissing his feet as everyone stares in disbelief.

Then the host of the party says, "If this man were a prophet, He would know what kind of woman is touching Him. She's a sinner!" He then says to Simon that He has something to say to him. Now, all eyes are on Jesus. What is He going to say? What is He going to do? Everyone is on the edge of their seats. They haven't seen some good drama like this in a long time. In classic Jesus form, He begins to tell a story. He was about to set up Simon and drop some wisdom. He shared, "A man loaned money to two people – 500 pieces of silver to one and 50 pieces to the other. But neither of them

16

could repay him, so he kindly forgave them both, cancelling their debts. Who do you suppose loved him more after that?' Simon answered, 'I suppose the one for whom he canceled the larger debt.' 'That's right,' Jesus said. Then He turned to the woman and said to Simon, 'Look at this woman kneeling here…'" Have you ever had someone talk to you, but they weren't looking at you? This is what Jesus was doing at this point. He then says, "Look at this woman…" I think there may have been some people in the crowd who still didn't get it at this point and thought that maybe Jesus was going to say something negative about the woman, but he actually does just the opposite.

Have you ever been to someone's home and they said or did something awkward that made you feel uncomfortable? I have experienced this before, but since it was their home, I just stayed quiet and didn't say anything. I just figured I wasn't going to come back again. Well, Jesus didn't stay quiet. He actually put Simon on blast in his own home. "When I entered your home, you didn't offer me water to wash the dust from my feet, but she has washed them with her tears and wiped them with her hair. You didn't greet me with a kiss, but from the time I first came in, she has not stopped kissing my feet. You neglected the courtesy of olive oil to anoint my head, but she has anointed my feet with rare perfume." Remember all those Jewish hospitality customs I mentioned? Jesus pointed out how He was denied each of them. This would have been considered disgraceful, as taking care of guests and honoring them was so important in their culture. Then Jesus tied in the story about the man who loaned two people money with the woman who showed him hospitality. "I tell you, her sins – and they are many – have been forgiven, so she has shown me much love. But a person who is forgiven little shows only little love." Boom! Once again, He is putting Simon and now the other Pharisees out there as He says the woman was forgiven many sins, and she is grateful and shows much love. But Simon and his squad think that they are all good. They don't ask for much forgiveness because they think they don't need it. As a result of their arrogance, they show little love.

If it couldn't get any more intense, Jesus still had one more bomb to drop. Then He turned to the woman and said to her, "Your sins are forgiven." This set off several people at the party, saying, "Who does He think He is, forgiving sins?" Jesus made the town prostitute the star of this passage. She was an outsider. People had given up on her. Simon and his guests and half the village didn't want her at the dinner party. Jesus not only called Simon out and condemned him for not offering him the customary hospitality, but he lifted up this woman and applauded her actions. He esteemed a woman at a predominantly male gathering. All of this was extremely counter-cultural. He showed love to the loveless. Let's follow his example.

LOVE LESSON:

Even in the midst of tension, Jesus showed love to those without a voice.

LOVE QUESTION:

Who are the people in your community without a voice, and how could you serve them?

LOVE APPLICATION:

How can you apply this devotional to your life?

16

LOVE NOTES:

What stuck out to you?

What else is God saying to you?

LOVE
our
City

DAY

17

OUR DOCTOR

"Healthy people don't need a doctor – sick people do."
— Matthew 9:12 NLT

"Now He's given me vision – Now he's given me drive / Now 24/7 you'll find me on the grind / Rhyming & Writing & Preaching & Reaching the Lost / Living & Breathing & Eating & Reppin' The Cross"

"HUSTLE – LEGACY REMIX" - URBAN D. FEAT. KB & LEGACY (HUSTLE EP)

17

The gospel of Matthew, chapter 9, tells a story of how Jesus walked up to a tax collector's booth and invited Matthew to become His disciple. Matthew jumped up and followed Him. This would have seemed absolutely crazy to anyone alive at that time. Tax collectors were the most hated people around. They were Jews who collected taxes for the oppressive Roman Empire. They were traitors. These tax collectors had a set amount they had to collect for Rome, and the rest they could keep. They made themselves rich off the hard work of their fellow Jews. Tax collectors were basically like the mafia of Jesus's time. If you didn't pay whatever price they set for your taxes, they could have you thrown in jail by the authority of the Roman government. It was basically legalized extortion. So, why in the world would Jesus want to invite one of those thieving traitors to be part of His team? It doesn't seem like it would be popular with the public opinion. But Jesus never seemed to care much about what people thought. He was more concerned about what His Father thought.

So why did Matthew get up and follow Him so quickly? Because everyone there in Capernaum knew about the miracles Jesus had recently performed. But, beyond recognizing this guy with the local buzz, I believe he felt something and experienced something from Jesus that he never had before. It was His love and grace that others had not extended. Jesus looked at this hated tax collector with compassion. He saw his potential, and even though he had made mistakes, Jesus knew He could transform him and use him. Although Matthew might have been living a comfortable lifestyle, he was rejected and despised by everyone. The simple words of Jesus, "Follow me," cut straight to Matthew's heart. It was like a second chance at life. Matthew was called. Jesus's invitation was giving him a new family and a new future. Without a word, Matthew's heart said, "Yes! I'm down! Let's go!"

Matthew got so excited about his new relationship with Jesus and his new lifestyle that he wanted to tell all of his friends about it. This is a regular occurrence when you have someone discover the love of Christ. They get excited and want to tell others so they can also experience it. Many of you reading this can relate to this story, as that was you at one point in your spiritual journey. Many new Christians start out with lots of zeal to reach others around them and love their city. They also may have a lot of non-Christian friends, as Matthew had. Unfortunately, as time goes on, many Christians lose that young zeal, and eventually, most of the friends they have around them are Christians. Refer back to Day 1 and our comfort problem.

So Matthew was new to this Christian thing, and he was on fire. He had a plan. He was going to throw this big house party and have all the tax collectors, crooks, and shady business people invited. Then he was going to get Jesus to come and talk to them, and hopefully they could experience what he now had. We see this unfold in Matthew 9:10, "Later, Matthew invited Jesus and His disciples to his home as dinner guests, along with many tax collectors and other disreputable sinners." So Jesus and His squad pulled up to the party and were mixing it up with all of these characters. It doesn't mean they were getting drunk or participating in any of the sinful things that may have been happening, but they were there among the people. Jesus was into building bridges and not barriers. Imagine if more Christians followed the example of Matthew and threw a house party for their non-Christian friends and had some Christian friends in the mix to show them the love of Jesus. Verse 11 reveals that Jesus was quickly criticized by religious people, as it says, "But when the Pharisees saw this, they asked His disciples. 'Why does your teacher eat with such scum?'" So Jesus was being judged just because He was around these people. As you love your city, there may be some religious people who may question why you would even put yourself in a situation where you are around certain kinds of people.

I love Jesus's reply. This is my favorite part: "Healthy people don't need a doctor – sick people do. Now go and learn the meaning of this scripture: 'I want you to show mercy, not offer sacrifices.' For I have come to call not those who think they are righteous, but those who know they are sinners." Drop the mic! The first part is super easy to literally understand. Jesus is hanging out with the spiritually sick people because they need a spiritual doctor. The second part gets a little deeper as He quotes Hosea 6:6, which is a passage calling Israel to repentance. It says, "I want you to show love, not offer sacrifices. I want you to know me more than I want burnt offerings." God doesn't want a routine sacrifice or a meaningless offering. He wants us to really get to know Him personally, and when we do, we will become like Him, and we will show love like Him. We'll show love to the hated. We'll show love to the unlovable. We'll be able to love our city through His eyes of compassion.

Again and again, we see Jesus go after the outsiders. They are the neighbors that everyone has written off. I've heard it said before that if you go after the people that no one wants, you will end up with the people everyone wants. It sounds like an oxymoron, but I've seen it play out like that so many times in my own ministry over the years. We've always reached out to the urban community that is predominantly unchurched and de-churched. Many of them have lots of issues and baggage. Some of them have church hurt and trust issues. Some of them have no church etiquette. Some of them are very unstable financially, emotionally, and relationally. It can be hard to love people like this, but if you look throughout the gospels, these are the exact people Jesus poured into. Even Jesus' disciples were a squad of misfits. But they were the ones who ended up changing the world. Peter and John stood before the court system of their day in Acts 4. The members of the council were astonished by the knowledge and the way they articulated themselves. How did they become so wise and confident? The second part of Acts 4:13 says, "They recognized them as men who had been with Jesus."

If you can get your neighbors with issues to spend time with Jesus, it changes the game. They begin to transform. We've watched some of the most challenging people become incredible leaders, passionate volunteers, generous givers, strategic entrepreneurs, gifted mentors, and the list goes on and on. We can rally an army of volunteers to participate in loving our city because they directly experienced the love of Christ from us. Now they want to give back and have other neighbors experience it too.

LOVE LESSON:

Jesus hung out with sinners.

LOVE QUESTION:

Who could you invite over to a house party that doesn't know Jesus?

LOVE APPLICATION:

How can you apply this devotional to your life?

LOVE NOTES:

What stuck out to you?

What else is God saying to you?

LOVE
our City

DAY 18

OUR DIVERSITY

"After this, I saw a vast crowd, too great to count from every nation and tribe and people and language, standing in front of the throne and before the lamb. "
— Revelation 7:9 (a) NLT

"I am the church, You are the church / We are the Church – since our Spiritual Rebirth / It ain't the building, It ain't the steeple / Look at the Biblical context – it's the people!"

"CHURCH" - URBAN D. (UN.ORTHODOX ALBUM)

18

The church in America has been in decline for several decades. There are several different statistics out there. Most of us are in the range that 65% - 85% of churches in America are either plateaued or declining [1]. I am not trying to be a downer, I'm actually an optimist, but I'm also a realist. Yes, we have turned a corner, and there has been a new surge of people going back to church. There is a new hunger, and people are searching and open to the gospel more than they have been in decades. There are lots of churches that are growing and thriving, but we still have to face the brutal fact that the average church in the West is struggling. The big question is why? There are lots of different factors and research that show it is a combination of things: breakdown of the family, a more secular agenda in education and entertainment, outdated approaches of churches, different sources where people get their spirituality, and the list goes on and on. Why are some churches growing, and most are plateaued or declining? There are many reasons, but I believe one of the greatest ones is that many churches have looked inward and moved into self-preservation mode. In this chapter, we'll focus on a few things that we've learned at our church, along with several other churches we work with. These are some critical areas that are helping us effectively reach our community, grow, and become healthier.

It can be challenging for many Christ-followers and churches to fully love their city when 75% of churches fail to have at least 20% diversity in their membership. Churches are 10 times more segregated than the neighborhoods they are in and 20 times more segregated than the nearby public schools [2]. This is one of the major reasons the church hasn't often been invited to the table to speak on issues of racism, classism, and discrimination that we see flooding the daily news headlines. Many think the church has no credibility to speak on these topics, as we are one of the most segregated institutions in our country. Yet, the Bible tells us we are called to be agents of reconciliation.

Research shows that many of younger generations are uncomfortable with the lack of diversity in churches. Dave Travis, the former CEO of Leadership Network, said, "Younger generations have come of age with diversity as an expected condition. If they look around and see a homogeneous congregation, they tend to discount the effectiveness of the church experience." Younger generations live in diversity, and when many of them step into a church, and everyone looks the same, it feels really weird. The church I lead is made up of people mostly under 40 years old. One consistent comment that people make is how they love the diversity at our church. Our church reflects our city. We must intentionally make changes so our churches can look more like the communities around them. It must go farther then just putting a few

token people on the platform. There must be diversity at the leadership table helping make decisions. These different perspectives are critical to help churches navigate language, responses, and even illustrations in the polarized world that we currently live in.

We shouldn't strive to become more diverse because it is now trending. This was Jesus' heart long before it became culturally popular. This was always His plan as he told the disciples to go and make disciples of all nations. The New Testament churches were reflective of their communities. Of the nine churches in the book of Acts, seven were multi-ethnic. The other two were not because they were in mono-ethnic communities.

When we think about the New Testament church, we can quickly think about the church in Jerusalem that started in Acts chapter 2 on the day of Pentecost. That first day alone, it grew to 3,000 people. Many of those people spoke different languages and were from different countries, as they were in the city to celebrate the festivals. The first day of the first New Testament church was multi-ethnic and multi-lingual. There are several other passages in the book of Acts that talk about thousands more being added to the church in Jerusalem on several occasions. But they weren't the most influential church in the New Testament.

The church in Antioch sent out the most missionaries

and made the largest impact. They were the church that commissioned and sent out Paul and others to spread the gospel on missionary journeys. Their church was multi-ethnic, multi-generational, and multi-class. It all started with their leadership team. It must always start from the top down. Maybe you have never noticed the beginning of Acts chapter 13. "Among the prophets and teachers of the church at Antioch of Syria were Barnabas, Simeon (called "the black man"), Lucius (from Cyrene), Manaen (the childhood companion of King Herod Antipas), and Saul." Barnabas was a Levite from Cyprus, which is an island in the Mediterranean. Simeon has a Jewish name, but he was called Niger, which literally meant black, because of his darker complexion. He was most likely of African descent. He was a Black Jew. Lucius was from Cyrene, which is the capital of Libya in North Africa. Manaen was a Jew raised with Herod the Great. The pastoral leadership team of the church of Antioch was multi-ethnic. You had European/Mediterranean (Barnabas), African (Simeon, Lucius), and Middle Eastern (Manaen, Saul). The leadership of the church of Antioch reflected the ethnic and cultural diversity of the city of Antioch.

When the leadership team is diverse, you will usually find that their mission strategy is more diverse. They care about reaching people who are from their background, and there is a greater awareness of various people groups right in their own community and abroad that need to hear about the love

of Christ. The church I lead is far from perfect, but we excel in diversity. Our staff, leadership, and volunteer teams are all diverse across the board. In our early days, much of this was organic, as many of us grew up in diverse urban environments. Diversity happened more naturally. Our church has always had some Hip-Hop/R&B flavor in our worship services, so that automatically attracted a diverse crowd. But as we grew in size and in our theology, we became more intentional. Our studies led us to see an even stronger case for church diversity in the scripture. This is one of our church's 7 core values. We regularly celebrate it and teach and preach it. Becoming and/ or balancing a diverse church is not always easy, as there are many different views, traditions, preferences, and politics in the congregation. If you'd like to learn more about this, I highly recommend Mark DeYmaz's book "Building a Healthy Multi-Ethnic Church.

LOVE LESSON:

New Testament churches were reflective of their communities.

LOVE QUESTION:

What are some reasons that churches in your community may be struggling?

LOVE APPLICATION:

How can you apply this devotional to your life?

LOVE NOTES:

What stuck out to you?

What else is God saying to you?

DAY 19

OUR WHY

"Instead, you must worship Christ as Lord of your life. And if someone asks about your hope as a believer, always be ready to explain it." — 1 Peter 3:15 NLT

"We live in the most advanced culture this planet has ever seen / But it's unheard / That's absurd / Man how could it be? / It's the powers that be / Broadband and 5G / That reach right into your home, your pocket, your screen"

"UN.HEARD" - URBAN D. (UN.HEARD ALBUM)

A s we love our city, it is important that we know the why. It is important that leaders equip their churches to understand the theology behind it. We can't assume everyone gets it. It is important that believers seek out resources and tools to sharpen their faith. The word "love" and the concept of loving other people are very fluid in our pluralistic culture. If we aren't careful, our outreach efforts can turn into a social justice effort that is void of the gospel. We closely monitor our "seed planting" approach with love for our city, as we don't want it to slip into a community service project with no spiritual purpose. Addressing this is regularly on the menu at our church. We are also intentional in preaching a series leading up to Love Our City Week, so we can biblically break down why we are doing it. We have done several "Love Our City" series at our church. The latest one is available for you to watch on our YouTube channel (crossover813). Plus, we released the outlines, transcripts, artwork, and small group videos and curriculum so other churches can use them and tweak them for their context. You may currently be going through the series at your church, as we have a lot of churches joining us in the Love Our City movement.

People are receiving more information than they ever have in the history of civilization. The growth in the internet, TV channels, and smartphones means that we now receive five times as much information as we did in 1986 [1]. But that pales in comparison to the growth in the amount of information we produce through our email, text, and social media platforms. Everyday the average person produces six newspapers' worth of information compared with just two and a half pages just a few decades ago. That's nearly a 200-fold increase [2]. People need filters more than ever for all the information being consumed and produced. We need the why. We need solid teaching and theology to help us stay on track in a world full of counterfeit gospels.

I'm a strong advocate for apologetics (learning to defend your faith). Growing up in the church has made me realize that the church overall has done a poor job of equipping people to be able to articulate why they believe what they believe. We live in an age where everyone questions everything. I don't think that is necessarily bad, but the danger is that people can now look in so many different places for answers. Many people ask Google before they ask God. They call Chat before they call Christ. We must prepare ourselves and believers in our churches with the right answers and the right information. 1 Peter 3:15 tells us, "Instead, you must worship Christ as Lord of your life. And if someone asks about your hope as a believer, always be ready to explain it."

Our church is intentional in offering apologetics classes, resources, and even a Sunday message series in our annual

calendar. Many of our series present how we got the Bible, how we know it hasn't been changed, and that we can trust it. We share evidence through history and archeology. We share how we can reason and find proof that brings us to an intellectual decision that the resurrection of Jesus really took place. We have also done several series that simply answered questions. Our church did a series entitled "You asked for it. People emailed their questions about God, the Bible, and how that connects to our everyday lives. It was powerful as we were able to bring up "touchy" issues, because they asked for it! They wanted to know what God's word really said about it. Of course, when you talk about hot-topic issues, you must always approach them with love, grace, and humility.

A few years ago, I had the opportunity to travel with a group of Christian leaders and apologists to Israel. It was my first time visiting the Holy Land, and it was absolutely amazing. I could write a book on just that. It was such a powerful experience that brought the Bible to life in new ways. I also learned so much about the Israeli and Palestinian conflict from people on both sides of it. What made it especially incredible was being on a trip with world-renowned apologetic authors and speakers whose material I regularly read and used. These guys are geniuses. The conversations were rich and enlightening. One of the guys on the trip, Sean McDowell, dropped a practical gem that sums up today's chapter: "No single apologetics or evangelism method works for everyone. People are different." As a believer, we must constantly strengthen our faith, add new tools, and sharpen the old ones. We must ask the Holy Spirit for discernment as we engage different people with different methods, sharing "our why".

LOVE LESSON:

We need solid teaching and apologetics to equip us in a world full of counterfeit gospels.

LOVE QUESTION:

When people ask you tough questions about God and the Bible, are you equipped to properly answer them.

LOVE APPLICATION:

How can you apply this devotional to your life?

LOVE NOTES:

What stuck out to you?

What else is God saying to you?

19

LOVE
our City

DAY

20

OUR RESPONSE

"Understand this, my dear brothers and sisters: You must be quick to listen, slow to speak and slow to get angry."
— James 1:19 NLT

"Everybody wants freedom, everybody wants change / We expect different - but we do the same thing / That defines insanity / We get depressed and question Christianity.

"FREEDOM" - URBAN D. (LOVE OUR CITY ALBUM)

20

What do we say when an unarmed Black man gets shot by White police officers? What do we say when George Floyd dies on camera for the world to see? What do we say when the former president has an assassination attempt on his life? When do we say when Roe Vs Wade gets flipped? What do we say after dozens of students get killed in a school shooting? These are critical moments that the church can and should speak into. Our church has not talked about every single event that has happened, because it seems there is something happening almost weekly. We never want that to overshadow the gospel, but we want to speak the gospel into those situations as often as possible. We can't ignore it as so many Christians and churches do, but what we say and how we say it are super important.

That's why I stress that having different ethnic groups at the leadership table is so critical. Our multi-ethnic, multi-generational, multi-class church has responded in a variety of ways over the past several years, and we've all learned some new things in our leadership meetings that have helped us address it even better. We've changed our direction a number of times due to new information and new perspectives that were presented as we planned, prepared, and prayed.

We must learn to listen. Most of us can grow in this area. When we hear about something or see something, we don't always respond as James 1:19 instructs us. We must remember that we haven't experienced what everyone else has. Although I may have experienced some discrimination in my life, it is nothing like what a 75-year-old African American man in my church has been through. We all have lenses that determine how we look at things. They are shaped by our life experiences. When we start a relationship with Christ, we become part of His family, but that does not change the color of our skin or the experiences we have gone through. We must learn to listen to others with different experiences, ideas, and even political leanings. When we truly put ourselves in their shoes and empathize with them, it can be a game-changer.

In the summer of 2016, there were several incidents of police shooting unarmed black men, along with police being shot, widespread protests, and social media videos going viral. There was a lot of tension and fear in many communities. I wanted to call a town hall meeting with police officers, city leaders, and the community to talk about it in our city before something popped off. I first had a meeting with some of our leadership team. Several of us felt it could be great for our church people and, at the same time, be a powerful outreach to the community. One of the guys in that meeting was a leader of the NAACP in our city. He liked the idea, but warned us about some past issues that happened in our community that most likely would draw out a few disgruntled people who would seek to hijack the meeting. He saw this happen

at multiple events he had been a part of around the city. We were totally unaware of this possibility, but when he laid out the facts, we knew we had to tweak the plan and use wisdom. We decided to have it be an in-house family meeting, and instead of us doing it on a different day and inviting the community, we interrupted a message series and did it on Sunday morning in all three of our services.

We had a panel with a city of Tampa Police officer, a Hillsborough County Sheriff officer, our city council woman, our congressmen and our business district leader. Myself, and my executive pastor and I were bookends on the panel asking questions on behalf of our community and people. We did no promotion, besides a short Facebook live post that morning. Channel 10 News immediately called us asking if they could come. Who knew the local news was following our Facebook page? I think churches many times underestimate their influence. We agreed to let the news come with the stipulation that they could only interview people we chose. We were not going to let them walk around our lobby and ask questions to random people. The panel went incredible and the unexpected news story also came out great. When you have the right people around your leadership table, and you are guided by God's spirit, some real God moments can occur.

There are a variety of other ways our church has addressed current issues in culture. Sometimes it was simply acknowledging what happened and praying for justice and peace in a service or on social media. Other times it was woven into a sermon. Sometimes it was an entire message. Several years ago, we did a series called "Fake News," and we played off of that popular term at the time and talked about fake news that is said about the Bible and Christianity. One of the week's titles was – "Fake News: The Bible supports slavery and White supremacy". We went into detail about the context of slavery in the scripture and talked about the differences between Old Testament slavery, colonial slavery, and modern-day slavery. We also addressed the bad theology that was formerly taught about the curse of Noah's son Ham. In the past, some churches, seminaries, and even Study Bibles taught that because of what happened in this passage, all dark-skinned people were cursed and would be servants. Unfortunately, this passage was wrongly used to justify slavery in the past. Black people, White people, and people of every shade were happy to see their church addressing it and explaining it in a balanced way. These are issues that every church may not want to talk about, but we need to find space to address it. There are more and more attacks from culture against the Bible and the church. They seek to discredit Christianity. With all the false narratives out there, it's so important that we educate our people with the truth so we can have a proper response.

LOVE LESSON:

We must respond with discernment and learn to listen to the Holy Spirit as we learn to listen to other people's perspectives.

LOVE QUESTION:

Have you had an experience in which you may have responded incorrectly in the past? What did you learn?

LOVE APPLICATION:

How can you apply this devotional to your life?

LOVE NOTES:

What stuck out to you?

What else is God saying to you?

LOVE
our City

DAY

21

OUR FLAVOR

"Taste and see that the Lord is good. Oh, the joys of those who take refuge in him!" — Psalm 34:8 NLT

"Like some Pollo (Chicken) straight off the grill / La palabra de Dios (The word of God) always gives you a balanced meal / That's seasoned with love like Adobo / That why we take this message global / Actions speak louder than vocals / I pray you see our actions clearer than bi-focals"

"LOVE REVOLUTION" - URBAN D. FEAT. D MAUB & K DRAMA (UN.HEARD ALBUM)

21

You have flavor! Embrace it and celebrate it! Each of you reading this has a unique spice to you. Nobody in the world has your DNA, fingerprint, or exact mix of skills, passions, and life experience. God created you that way. You have some special gifts and talents that he has blessed you with, so you could use them to give others a taste of God's love. Jesus told us in Matthew 5:13 that we are the salt of the earth. He meant that His disciples' good deeds would have a huge positive impact in the world around them for the glory of God. Now, with this declaration, there was also a warning. Jesus told us to be careful that we don't lose our flavor. He makes the point that without our flavor, we can become useless, like the lukewarm water we talked about in Day 1. Some of you may have lost some of your flavor, but I believe that God is going to use love for our city to revive some of your gifts, talents, and calling.

Crossover Church has been taught to love our city through our everyday lifestyles. In addition, there are weekly programs and monthly outreach events for our church family to plug into and show love. One of the biggest impacts has been the "Love Our City Week, where the majority of the church volunteers to complete community service projects in the district around the church. We are also joined by hundreds of business partners, ministries, and residents who volunteer with us. We are in a very diverse area, so our strategy is to reach as many different people groups as possible. Our leadership team put up a whiteboard and made categories of different tribes in our neighborhood. As we came up with project ideas, we put them in those categories. The demographics in our district include college students, business people, single mothers, first responders, teachers, families in poverty, immigrants, retired people, tourists, and the homeless. Some of these people live in our community, some of them work here, and some of them play here. Either way, we want to intentionally find ways to give them a taste of the love of Christ through tangible acts of kindness.

Hosting a Love Our City week or a one-day outreach is a great way to also give people a taste of serving. Most people are already busy and overwhelmed in their daily lives. When they hear about opportunities to get involved in a consistent serving position at a church or a non-profit, many can quickly write it off, as they feel they just don't have time. Of course, we will always find time for the things we think are truly important. Creating a one-time opportunity for people to serve can be much more attractive and can open the door for people to put their toe in the water. We've found that if they have a good experience when they serve, it is something that quickly moves up on their priority list. We've witnessed many people start serving consistently after their participation in Love Our City Week. We had several people who served on a project and loved it so much that they became a part of our city planning team.

If you are reading this and you are not regularly serving at your local church in some capacity, I pray this book will nudge you to move into the right fit that God has for you. It can be tempting to think that your church doesn't need you, or God can't use you, but don't fall for that lie. You are not reading this book by accident. If you got all the way to Day 21, God wants to use you to love your city in unique ways that he created you. I challenge you to get off the bench and bring your flavor to the game!

LOVE LESSON:

You have some special gifts and talents that God has blessed you with, so you could use them to give others a taste of his love.

LOVE QUESTION:

How are you regularly giving people a taste of God's love?

LOVE APPLICATION:

How can you apply this devotional to your life?

LOVE NOTES:

What stuck out to you?

What else is God saying to you?

LOVE our City
WEEK 3 VIDEO SERIES

PLAY VIDEO

1. Our neighbors have all kinds of _____,
but yet all kinds of _____.
As our character becomes more like Christ – our vision
_____ and we can begin to see
people and situations the way that Jesus sees them.

* Gospel of John Chapter 8

2. Example after example we see Jesus offering radical
_____; from the woman at the well
with 5 husbands, to Matthew the hated tax collector,
to the town prostitute at Simon's dinner party.

3. The WHY is super important. Sometimes
we forget to answer the WHY and we just
want to jump into the _____.

"And if someone asks about your hope as a believer,
always be ready to explain it. But do this in a gentle
and respectful way." — 1 Peter 3:15-15 NLT

4. We should never look to start a fight or
win a debate, but to respectfully engage with
people and explain the _____.

"I am the way, the truth, and the life. No one can come
to the Father except through me." — John 14:6 NLT

DISCUSSION QUESTIONS

1. In what ways has God changed your vision
in how you see people and situations?

* Read the Gospel of John 8:1-11

2. Has someone ever shown you grace (given you
something you didn't deserve)? What happened?

* Read 1 Peter 3:15-16

3. Have you ever had someone ask you a spiritual question and
you didn't know the answer, or you struggled to explain it?

4. Has someone asked you a spiritual question
and you were able to explain it well?

5. What are some of the fake gospels or false
religions that may be popular in your city?

6. Are you confident enough in your faith to have a
conversation with someone from a different religion?

DAY

22

OUR ATMOSPHERE

"Even though I am a free man with no master, I have become a slave to all people to bring many to Christ."
— 1 Corinthians 9:19 NLT

"Between us and God there was a rift / Because us and sin kissed / We couldn't resist / We took an L and missed / We were separated from our creator because God and sin can't co-exist / But Jesus brought a SHIFT!

"NEW COMMUNITY" - URBAN D.

22

We have the ability and the responsibility to change the atmosphere. If you are a Christ-follower, you have the Holy Spirit living in you. He can empower you in every situation you enter. Many of us regularly enter drama-filled environments at work, school, or home. We can change the atmosphere. It may not be easy. It may be met with resistance. It may take time. But God can use us to bring a shift and set a new tone. I've watched this happen time and time again when a Christ-follower would start working in a new position, start attending a new school, or start playing on a new team. I've watched it happen with a new believer who would begin to change the atmosphere in their home as their walk with Christ grew stronger. Just recently, a brother started attending our church and gave his life to Christ, got baptized, and led his wife and kids to church, then his uncles and his mom. The entire atmosphere in his family shifted radically from just a year ago.

We have to learn to read the atmosphere as we step into it so we can better serve. This was Paul's strategy as he shared in 1 Corinthians chapter 9:19-22, "Even though I am a free man with no master, I have become a slave to all people to bring many to Christ. When I was with the Jews, I lived like a Jew to bring the Jews to Christ. When I was with those who follow the Jewish law, I too lived under that law. Even though I am not subject to the law, I did this so I could bring to Christ those who are under the law. When I am with the Gentiles who do not follow the Jewish law, I too live apart from that law so I can bring them to Christ. But I do not ignore the law of God; I obey the law of Christ. When I am with those who are weak, I share their weakness, for I want to bring the weak to Christ. Yes, I try to find common ground with everyone, doing everything I can to save some."

As you step into different spaces, there will be different ways to talk and respond in order to become an atmosphere changer. I've had to learn this over the years as I started as a youth pastor and a Hip-Hop artist. I was predominantly working with teenagers. Eventually, I got pushed into being the lead pastor at my church. I had to learn to become a better communicator with adults. It was different, but I learned how to still be myself. There are times when I'm in the hood with neighborhood residents, while there are times I'm in the board room with business leaders. Sometimes I'm wearing jeans and a T-shirt, while other times I'm throwing on a blazer on top of that T-Shirt to dress it up. I'm still being myself, but I've learned how to change language so I can communicate with different people groups and change the atmosphere in our diverse city.

Paul also learned to read the atmosphere when he first went to Athens. When he first got there, he was deeply disturbed by the spiritual environment. People were far from God, and the city was full of idols. The scripture tells us that he

took some time and studied the people, spoke to the locals, and tried to read the temperature of the culture. Once he got his bearings, he started to turn up the heat. He gathered a large crowd where everybody went to politic and debate. Acts 17:22-23 in the Message version says, "So Paul took his stand in the open space at the Areopagus and laid it out for them. 'It is plain to see that you, Athenians, take your religion seriously. When I arrived here the other day, I was fascinated by all the shrines I came across. And then I found one inscribed, to the god nobody knows. I'm here to introduce you to this God so you can worship intelligently, know who you're dealing with.'" Paul drew them in with something familiar from their culture. A little farther down in the passage, he even quoted one of their poets. If Paul were here today, he might be quoting a chart-topping rapper. At the end of his presentation, there were some who laughed, some who said they wanted to hear more, and some who became believers that day. Paul didn't just take the temperature; he became the thermostat and turned up the heat, and several people became part of the church in that city.

In 2010, our church retrofitted a 43,000 square foot former Toys R' Us store in the heart of Tampa's urban community. Many of the stores fled to the new malls that were built in the suburbs. The neighborhood's nickname was Suitcase City due to its transient nature. The poverty rate in the immediate neighborhood was the highest in the city. It wasn't a good neighborhood to move a church into, but we knew we were called there to change the environment and set a new atmosphere. At first, it seemed overwhelming as there were so many needs and the problems were so layered and complex. But we just kept seeking God's plan, loving people, meeting needs, and making disciples. But fifteen years into it, we've seen a dramatic shift. There is a lot of work to do, but the change is happening.

Love our city is an atmosphere-changing event in our community. We unleash over 1,000 volunteers into our neighborhood. As they are serving people all week long, it shifts the tone. Get ready, as doing Love our city will change the atmosphere in your hood. God will work in your people, through your people, and on the people they serve.

LOVE LESSON:

We have to learn to read every atmosphere we step into, so we can serve in a greater way.

LOVE QUESTION:

What is the temperature for God in your neighborhood, workplace, school, and church? How can you become more of a thermostat and turn up the heat?

LOVE APPLICATION:

How can you apply this devotional to your life?

LOVE NOTES:

What stuck out to you?

What else is God saying to you?

DAY

13

OUR REPUTATION

"Your love for one another will prove to the world that you are my disciples." — John 13:35 NLT

"We've been empowered, so we empower others / Fathers, and Mothers, Sisters and Brothers, Haters and Lovers / The haters they love us - once they discover / And see - there's no blindness / We loving our city with acts of that kindness.

"LOVE OUR CITY 1.0" - URBAN D. (LOVE OUR CITY ALBUM)

13

Your reputation matters. It's a big deal. Our reputation as followers of Jesus matters. Even if your church doesn't have a reputation... the capital C church does. What is that reputation? It depends on who you talk to. Some people love the church, others are indifferent about it, and some have strong feelings against it. There are many people who pass by your church each day and have no idea what actually goes on inside. They have never been inside, and a lot of them don't plan to ever come. Some people have never been to church, while others have left and don't have plans to return. There is a negative narrative that many people have about the church. We have a bad reputation in some people's eyes. They may think the church is only about money, or rules, or judgment, or politics. Love Our City is all about changing that narrative. When we get out of the seats and into the streets, we can change people's perception of Christians and the church. They can experience the love of Christ, and this can be a catalyst to change their life forever. This will not only enhance your church's reputation, but also the church as a whole.

Our church has grown in size, influence, and impact because of our reputation for loving our city. When something good is happening, people will talk about it. When people want to do something in your community, they usually want to talk with the community anchors. We have watched this happen as our reputation grew. Our church has been approached to partner with multiple major organizations in our community, including the city of Tampa. Why did this happen? They kept saying, "I'm hearing about all the great things you are doing for our community." This would be followed up by them thanking us and saying they wanted to work with us.

Our city was impacted by Hurricane Irma in September of 2017 and Hurricane Helene in 2024. Fortunately, our church was in one of the few places that still had power. We sprang into action to love our city and provide hurricane relief from our location. The local business alliance, partners, and the city partnered with us and helped spread the word. Our site became the official hurricane relief efforts of North Tampa. We served hundreds of families and gave away tons of supplies. The mayor, city council, and FEMA asked to set up a town hall meeting at our church a few weeks after the storm in 2024 to address relief efforts. We hosted the meeting with hundreds of residents and every media station from the city was present. The mayor asked me to welcome everyone, open with a prayer, and introduce her.

Over the years, I've been invited to attend several private business leader events where I was the only pastor in the room. They wanted me in the room because they like what our church is doing, and they want to partner with us. We've had government agencies support our Back 2 School Jam.

We've had corporations write us significant checks for Love Our City. We've been invited to sit on boards making major decisions that are reshaping our community. We are regularly asked to open our city council meetings in prayer. These doors have opened because of our approach. We are here to love and serve our city. When you consistently do that, people will notice. There are some strategic things you can do that I talk about in the leader's guide, but a lot of this will organically begin to happen.

At the end of Love Our City week, we throw a big party. When is the party? It's at our Sunday services. We don't create a separate event; we want them to come and experience our Sunday services and see what we are really all about. We have incredible worship, a highlight video from the week, a creative message, photo booths, and more. We see hundreds of people who we touched come out to our services. It's a big celebration where we clearly share the gospel and talk about the love of Christ. Our rhythm is doing love our city, two weeks before Easter Sunday. We've found that gives us even more momentum, as it engages our people to invite others at their jobs, schools, and neighborhoods. This past Easter, we had the largest attendance in our history, and over 100 people indicated they started a relationship with Christ by filling out a card and receiving a free copy of my book "Next Steps on Your Spiritual Journey". We followed up with all of those people, and a few Sundays after Easter, we had 104 people get baptized.

There are no strings attached with love our city, as people don't have to do anything now or ever to receive the blessing we are giving them. But we are intentional in inviting them to the party. Every time we do an outreach event, we are always putting something in their hand inviting them to what is next. It's totally up to them if they come. We are planting seeds and praying that God will move in their hearts. Our reputation strategy is to build a relationship with them and continue to cultivate that so they can get to know us and the God we love and serve.

LOVE LESSON:

When we get out of the seats and into the streets, we can change people's perception of Christians and the church.

LOVE QUESTION:

What is the reputation of Christians and churches in your city? How do you think a Love Our City Week could impact it?

LOVE APPLICATION:

How can you apply this devotional to your life?

LOVE NOTES:

What stuck out to you?

What else is God saying to you?

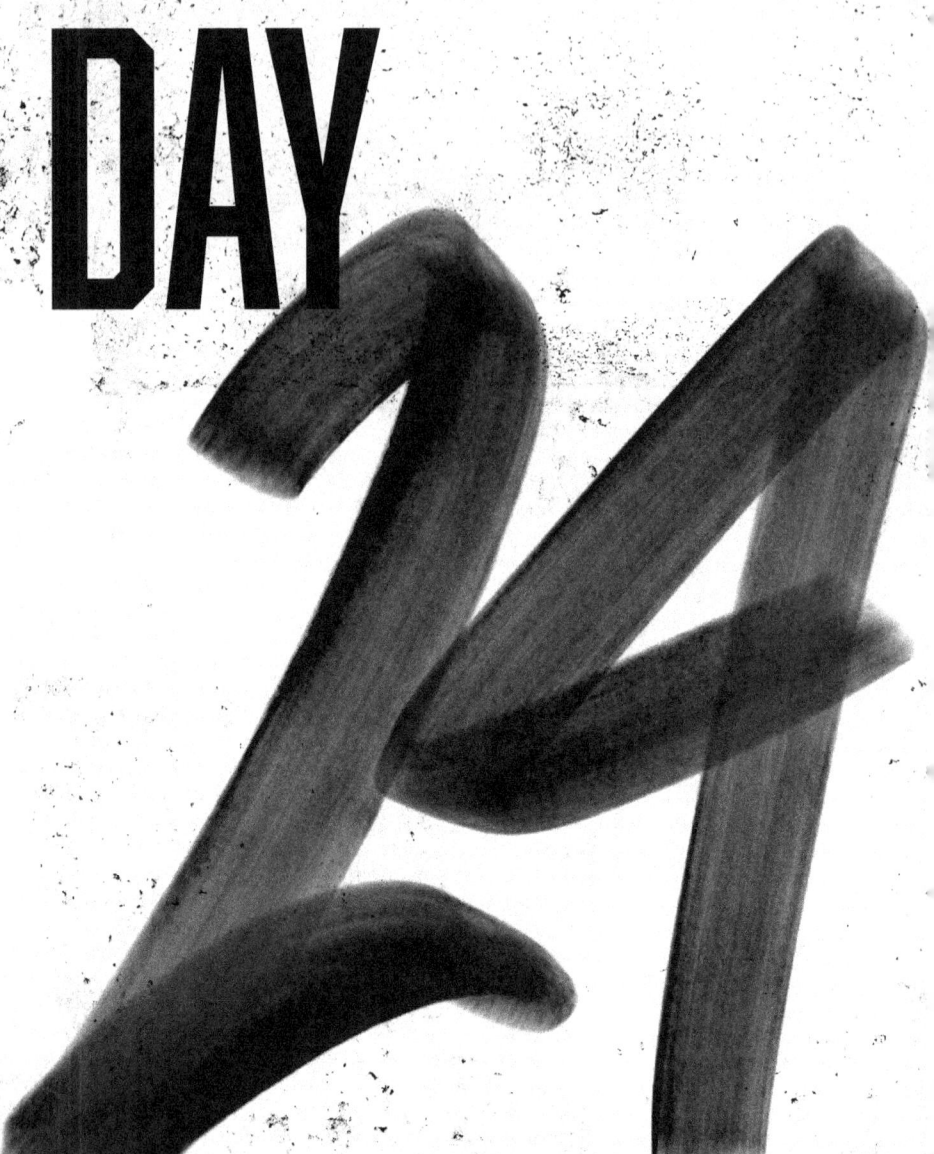

DAY 24

OUR PRAYER

"After sending them (the crowd) home, he (Jesus) went up into the hills by himself to pray. Night fell while he was there alone." — Matthew 14:23 NLT

"I never start moving until I pray / Sparking evidently at the top of the day / I'm gathering wisdom for the words to say / Show the way / Map the play / Okay!"

"HUSTLE" - URBAN D. (UN.ORTHODOX ALBUM)

efore, during, and after, we love our city; we should pray. This was a model that Jesus set for us. During his three and a half years of ministry, he was incredibly busy, but there were several times recorded in the gospels where he broke away from the crowd to get alone and pray. There were times when it was early in the morning before his ministry launched for the day, and other times when it was late at night after a long day of ministry. We can see several key moments throughout Jesus' life when he prayed: at his baptism, when he was choosing the disciples, when others were in need, at the last supper, in the garden of Gethsemane, and on the cross.

The gospels are full of lessons on prayer. Jesus taught us to pray without a desire to be seen (Matt. 6:5-6). He told us to reconcile with others before praying (Matt. 5:23-24). Jesus showed us how to pray before important decisions (Luke 6:12-13). He taught us not to pray with empty phrases (Matt. 6:7). Jesus also challenged us to be bold and believe that God will answer our prayers (Mark 11:24).

As you are gearing up to love your city, you need to get spiritually ready. We could have everything organized with community service projects, volunteers, and resources, but if we do it in our own strength and strategies, it will not have the impact it was meant to. We must intentionally get prayed up. It's important that we do this personally and corporately. Our church has put on lots of large events over the years, from outreaches to conferences. At some of these events we have hundreds of volunteers involved, and there are lots of moving parts. There have been times when, in our busyness, we didn't cover the event in prayer as we should have. In those events, we noticed it either didn't have the same spiritual impact, or there was an off vibe with some negativity or disorganization.

All of us have busy seasons in our lives. Those are the times we need to make sure that we spend consistent time communicating with our Creator. When our schedules are more packed than normal, it can put us in a vulnerable place as we are out of our normal rhythm. Sometimes those seasons can be draining, and other times those seasons can be exciting and full of momentum.

When you are working on something you are passionate about, it can be a lot of fun. I have to admit, as a leader, I love momentum. But momentum can be dangerous. It can make us think we are better than we are. It can hide our issues. It can even cause us to get prideful. The thing that will keep us grounded in busy seasons is prayer. No matter how busy we are, we have to carve

out time to spend with Jesus. That must become a non-negotiable in our lives.

Several years ago, I attended a business leaders' event that helped us set goals for the New Year. Each speaker who got up shared about their personal prayer and devotional time that they did each morning. I am an artist, so I'm more of a night person, so getting up earlier to pray didn't exactly fit my preference of later in the day. But God spoke to me that morning and challenged me to step into a more intimate prayer life in this new season. I knew it would stretch me, but I was hungry to get more intimate with God. Every morning, I get up and head over to my prayer closet and pull out my journal, and I write down a blessing for the day and number it.

This morning I recorded blessing #2,424. Then I pray, listen, read, and journal. Each year, I read through the Bible in a reading plan with a different translation. It has breathed new life into my relationship with Jesus that has now been over three decades. God will show Himself to you in deeper ways when you press in. If you don't already have a regular prayer and devotional rhythm, then you need to create one. If you do have one, God may switch it up and reorganize it as he did for me.

As you and your church or small group get ready to love your city, I encourage you to personally get prayed up and also spend some time together praying. Our church has a prayer meeting on the first Saturday of every month. When Love Our City Week happens, we pray for every single group before they engage in their community service project. Our leaders send them out with a blessing as everyone first meets in our church lobby to get their t-shirts, supplies, leaders, and teammates. I'm praying for every person who reads this book, every church that does love our city, and every person who gets touched by it. Let's go!

LOVE LESSON:

Jesus regularly broke away from the crowd to get alone to spend time in prayer.

LOVE QUESTION:

What does your regular prayer rhythm look like? How could you take it deeper?

LOVE APPLICATION:

How can you apply this devotional to your life?

LOVE NOTES:

What stuck out to you?

What else is God saying to you?

LOVE our City

DAY 25

OUR HAND-UP

"Share each other's burdens, and in this way obey the law of Christ. If you think you are too important to help someone, you are only fooling yourself. You are not that important." - Galatians 6:2-3 NLT

"Be like Christ and give a hand up / We gotta Love Our City - we gotta stand up / For the voiceless, those that are choiceness / All talk and no action is pointless.

"HAND UP" - URBAN D. (LOVE OUR CITY ALBUM)

We hand out a lot of things during Love Our City Week. It is an initial touch to our community. In many cases, it is meeting critical needs for people. But we don't want to stop at just a handout. We also want to give a hand up. Because they will need groceries next month, they will need more Christmas presents next December. They will need a backpack next school year, and they might get really upset if all the purple ones are gone. We have to be careful that we are not feeding a poverty mindset. If you only create constant systems where you are just giving things out, you can enable people to continue to stay in the same place. It can build entitlement and apathy. Our outreach leadership team promotes our regular outreach programs to different groups of people each month so we don't have as many repeats.

One of my favorite events our church hosts every year is called Affordable Christmas. For fourteen years, we have been partnering with a local non-profit called Current. We partner with several other local non-profits that are working with families who are struggling. Funds are raised, brand new toys are purchased, and our church gym becomes a toy store. The irony is that our church meets in a former Toys' R' Us store. So once a year, we turn it back into a toy store where parents can come and shop with dignity and get a hand up. Everyone loves to get a good deal and save money. We're not giving these toys away for free, but the prices are around 90% off the retail price. It creates some skin in the game and ownership that they bought these gifts and hand-picked them for their kids. There are only three price categories - $3, $5, and $10. Several families are walking out with brand new bikes or new tablets for just $10. The parents get hundreds of dollars worth of toys for $25 or $30. Plus, we wrap their gifts for them and serve them lunch. Someone didn't show up at their house, giving their kids free gifts; the parents were empowered to be the heroes, and the gifts were from them. This is a creative hand up.

You can't meet every type of need in the city. It's impossible. That's why it is so important to build partnerships with other organizations and ministries in your community that are giving a hand up. You don't need to duplicate services. In most communities, there are already some great programs to empower people. Find ways to support those organizations by serving them, funding them, and sending people their way. Of course, you need to vet them and make sure they are safe, run well, and not leading people down a different spiritual path. We don't have GED classes at our church, because there are several good ones in our neighborhood to which we refer people. We partner with several of our local Community Development Corporations to host job training classes and empowerment classes in our facility

and at their locations. We recently partnered with Better Together and hosted a job fair. We had 33 employers come and 22 resource agencies. We helped dozens of people get their resumes up to par. We had a bell set up that every time someone got a job, they rang the bell. That day, 81 people rang the bell! Plus, hundreds of interviews were set up for the weeks to follow. It was an amazing hand-up event that served over 500 people. Several people from our church family got new jobs. Research who is doing good work in your community and see how you can help each other. Research what the needs are in your community and where the gaps are. God may be calling you to start something new that fills a void.

Affordable housing has become a crisis in our community that has grown even more since the pandemic, as so many new people have moved to our city, and gentrification is happening in nearly every neighborhood. Our dream is for our love our city non-profit, to purchase some apartments and houses to help families in our church and in our community. In the meantime, we can still give a hand up as we have resources in our church community. Several people are in the real estate, credit repair, and mortgage fields. They got together and created a first-time home buyers class that we host quarterly. We have helped over a dozen families get their first home, and set up dozens of others on a pathway towards owning a home. Many times, people don't move forward because they are not exposed to the right information. We are passionate about helping our people get informed so they can take their next steps.

LOVE LESSON:

You can't just stop at a handout. You must meet deeper needs and give a hand up to help people become self-sustainable.

LOVE QUESTION:

What are some ways you, your family, your small group, or your church could help give people a "hand up" in your city?

LOVE APPLICATION:

How can you apply this devotional to your life?

LOVE NOTES:

What stuck out to you?

What else is God saying to you?

25

LOVE our City

DAY

26

OUR PARTNERSHIPS

"Two can accomplish more than twice as much as one, for the results can be much better." — Ecclesiastes 4:9 TLB

"We go together like chicken and teriyaki / Greeks and Soulvaki / Canadians and ice hockey / like helmets and Kawasaki / like vinyl and disc jockey / We go together like Philadelphia and Rocky"

"WE GO TOGETHER LIKE"- URBAN D. (TRANZLATION ALBUM)

I f you've read this far in the book, I know you are excited and ready to make an impact. You may have a lot of questions about the details and how to love our city in your community. It seems like a lot of work, and it is, but if you have systems in place, it can run smoothly no matter how large it grows. When you work together as a team, you can accomplish much more, like the scripture says, "Two can accomplish more than twice as much as one, for the results can be much better." We are not meant to do life and do ministry alone. Each of us has unique gifts, talents, and strengths. When we partner, there is so much more than we can accomplish as a team. You will be amazed at how much you can get done with a focused group of people.

Our church has been in our location for over fifteen years. We've built partnerships with several organizations to help make our community a better place. When the pandemic hit, several of our partners started calling us, asking us to partner with them to meet immediate needs in our part of the city. One of those partners was Feeding Tampa Bay. They are the largest food distribution non-profit in our metropolitan area. We have had a partnership with them for over a decade with our food pantry. Non-profits can purchase groceries from them for pennies on the dollar. When the pandemic hit, most of the food pantries across the city closed as they were run by retirees who were in the at-risk age category for the virus.

They knew our church was predominantly younger, and they asked if we could set up a grocery drive-thru outside in our parking lot. We said yes, but asked how much the food would cost as we had to figure out how to fund it. They told us all of the food was free. They already had funding for it and just needed a trusted partner that had young volunteers and a big parking lot.

We had a grocery drive-thru for fourteen months, serving up to 800 families a week. Many families would wait up to an hour in their cars in the parking lot in the hot Florida weather. We created a water bottle team that went around and served bottled water, talked with people, and offered prayer if the situation presented itself. For many people, this was the only interaction they had with real people during the pandemic, and it created some amazing ministry moments. About six months later, a lady came up to me in the church lobby after a service and said, "Hey! Are you the lead pastor here?" I said, "Yes." She said, "I thought that was you. You prayed for us in the grocery drive-thru and invited us to church. Today was my first time coming to church in twenty-one years. My name is Judi with an i (she pointed to her eye)."

Judi has now been attending our church for several years. She recommitted her life to Christ, got baptized, and started bringing her grandkids to church. Eventually, her son started coming to church, and he recently became a member.

26

This was all possible because of a partnership that we had to distribute food to families in need.

In 2024, Hurricane Helene slammed the Tampa Bay area. It was the worst hurricane I've experienced living in Florida over thirty years. Several of our partners came alongside us to help. One of those amazing partners was Good 4 Community. The CEO of their non-profit jumped in one of their buses with a few of their team and filled it with supplies. They drove for two days from Indiana to get there the day after the storm hit. We set up a big relief effort and fed over 500 people and gave away pallets of supplies. Good 4 Community was so impressed with our operation that he handed me the keys to the bus and asked me if we could use the bus. I said, "Absolutely, but what does the insurance on that cost?" He said, "Don't worry about it, you are one of our partners now, so we'll continue to keep it in our name and pay the insurance. Just send us your driver's information, and we'll add them to the policy." Wow! One of our partners blessed us with a bus that we now use to pick up food, supplies, and resources. We used to regularly spend hundreds of dollars to rent U-Haul trucks for big pick-ups, but now we just use our bus!

My friend Elisio has a huge passion for outreach and has built all kinds of partnerships over the years. At times, he gets so much stuff that he can't distribute all of it, so he shares the love with other churches and non-profits doing great work.

Elisio has become our Turkey partner as he has the hookup to supply us with turkeys to give away at Thanksgiving and Christmas. We, in turn, paid it forward and blessed a Spanish church with over a hundred turkeys so they could do their first outreach of this kind in another part of the city. At our location, we were able to bless hundreds and hundreds of families from our church and our community with a great meal for the holidays.

LOVE LESSON:

When we come together, there is so much more than we can accomplish as a team.

LOVE QUESTION:

What are some organizations in your city you could partner with?

LOVE APPLICATION:

How can you apply this devotional to your life?

LOVE NOTES:

What stuck out to you?

What else is God saying to you?

DAY 27

OUR STORIES

"In the same way, let your good deeds shine out for all to see, so that everyone will praise your heavenly Father." — Matthew 5:16 NLT

"It was a total eclipse / of the heart / brand new start / no more clips of the dark / my life was canvas and the creator was making beautiful art / Like a beautiful mark / Here's the beautiful part / I found true peace at home / True peace alone / True peace is known / When you find that Jesus Christ is on the throne"

"HOME" - URBAN D. (UN.ORTHODOX ALBUM)

27

There are so many God moments we've experienced from Love Our City Week and Love Our City projects throughout the year. We use these projects and events to plant seeds. We are simply following the words of Jesus, where we are taking care of the poor, the widows, and the orphans. We are giving a cup of cold water in his name (we literally have water bottle giveaways). Many times, we may not be the ones who see those seeds grow. But the more you keep loving your city, the more harvest you will begin to see unfold around you as the Holy Spirit begins to work in people's lives. We've seen lots of amazing stories, and we believe there are many seeds that are still in the germination process.

Jose came home from work and found his wife with a huge smile on her face as she shared about a church group that randomly brought a bag of groceries to their door that evening. She had been praying for a miracle as she was unsure how they would have enough food to make it through the week. God provided. The next day, Jose went to work at his maintenance job at the mall. A group of people showed up from this same church and had appreciation gift bags for all forty-five employees. The bag included a candy bar, some gum, a handwritten note, and a gift card for a sandwich. Nobody ever gave the maintenance men gift bags of appreciation. He was touched. Jose wanted to find out more about this church group and why they would do this.

Even though Jose didn't speak English fluently yet, he started attending our church.

Liz had been going through a rough season. She was at the gym when a young girl came up and invited her to the Love Our City celebration party coming up next Sunday. Liz had been thinking about going back to church, and this was a sign for her. When she showed up at Crossover Church that Sunday, she immediately felt welcomed, and God started doing something inside of her during the service. At the end, she responded to the gospel and made a commitment to get right with God. We were having a spontaneous water baptism that day, and I started sharing about making a public declaration of your faith through water baptism. She had never been baptized before, and she was not planning on it, but as people started standing up and going down front, she felt God's spirit pulling her, but she didn't move. I felt there were still a few more people who were going to respond, so we gave one more opportunity. Liz jumped out of her seat and ran down to the front as the church celebrated! She and 60 other people got baptized that Sunday. The next Sunday, she started bringing her friend Luis, who hadn't been to church in nearly two decades. They both went through the 3D Growth Track and officially became members. A few months later, Liz joined our worship team and was part of the team for many years before she moved to another city, where she continues to let her light shine.

Our bus blessing project goes to the bus terminal to give out a free one-day bus pass along with a gift bag. It was actually the very first project of Crossover's Love Our City Week 2018. So, we were all fired up and ready to reach people. There were so many people at the bus terminal that we were out of bus passes and gift bags in less than 15 minutes, but there were some God moments.

I met Derek from Miami. He was a middle-aged guy who had just moved to Tampa a few months ago. Although he was happy to get a bus pass and gift bag, he didn't seem very engaged at first. I asked a few questions about how he liked Tampa and what brought him here. He started to warm up and ask a few questions about what we were doing. I shared with him about the church, and eventually I told him I was the lead pastor. There was suddenly a shift in the conversation at that point as he started asking me some deep spiritual questions about struggling to let go and let God take control. Here we were at the bus terminal, and it was turning into this special ministry moment. I shared some of my spiritual journey and encouraged him. He grabbed my hand and said, "Thanks, Pastor, I'll see you at church on Sunday." Sure enough, that Sunday after service, he came up to me in the lobby and said, "Hey, you remember me?" Thank God I have a good memory (at least short-term), and I said, "Hey! It's Derek from Miami – you came!" He was blown away that I remembered him and talked about how much he enjoyed the service and that he found his new church home.

Jalisa is a millennial who kept getting invited to church by her supervisor, Jackson. She was hesitant as she hadn't been to church in a long time, and the last time she went, it was awkward. But when he invited her to come serve on his team for Love Our City Week, this sparked her interest. She went with a group to the laundromat and paid for everyone's laundry. Jalisa loved seeing the surprise on people's faces and the conversations that followed. She got to meet several other church members and even one of the pastors at the event. They made her feel like family. Jalisa was so curious about the church that she showed up at the celebration party and has regularly been attending ever since.

This past Sunday, I met Johnathan, who has been riding to church in his electric wheelchair scooter. He lives right down the street and rides to church on the sidewalk. He first came to the church last year when we served our community with hurricane relief efforts. His neighbor invited him, and they've been coming to church together ever since. Johnathan was so excited to tell me how the church has impacted his life and how he looks forward to coming every time the doors are open. When you love all of your city, your stories will become multi-generational, from college students to young families to senior citizens rolling in on an electric scooter.

LOVE LESSON:

The more you keep loving your city, the more harvest you will begin to see unfold around you as the Holy Spirit begins to work in people's lives.

LOVE QUESTION:

What is a great story of spiritual transformation that you have seen from showing the love of Christ to others?

LOVE APPLICATION:

How can you apply this devotional to your life?

LOVE NOTES:

What stuck out to you?

What else is God saying to you?

DAY 28

OUR MOVEMENT

"Feed the hungry, and help those in trouble. Then your light will shine out from the darkness, and the darkness around you will be as bright as noon." — Isaiah 58:10 NLT

"When rebuilding there's seasons of growth and forward movement / But there's times of plateau and decline that's not in your blueprint"

"REBUILDING MOVEMENT" - URBAN D. (REBUILD ALBUM)

Although I may have written the book about love our city, I'm not the one who originated the idea of churches serving their communities. Churches have been doing similar things like this for centuries. Like King Solomon said, "There is nothing new under the sun." We take ideas and remix them for our context. Over the years, we have seen several churches doing service projects, and we were inspired and put our own spin on it. One of the churches that inspired us was a church plant that our church helped mentor. They did a residency internship with us. Our church's innovative ideas have helped many up-and-coming churches.

As we help churches, they also help and inspire us. Their creativity and youthful zeal is contagious. They innovate and take big risks for God's kingdom. Jerome and Crystal Vierling planted "City Life Lansing" church in Lansing, Michigan. In 10 years they grew this amazing diverse church to over 600 weekly attenders in a portable location. As one of the spiritual overseers of the church I've been able to watch this journey from a front row seat.

They recently merged with "Trinity Church" and became "One Church." It's a really cool story of Rebuilding. I love their community as they go all in on loving their city.

Jerome Vierling – Founding Pastor of
City Life Church & Pastor of One Church

"We launched City Life Lansing, an inner-city church plant in Lansing, MI. Talk is cheap, and so many of our team know what it is like to feel forgotten. Our heartbeat is to let the city know that Jesus loves the city! In the early months, love the city was our anthem. In our first year, we kicked off a "Love the city week". We put a goal in our first year to raise $20,000 to do as many acts of love in one week. The problem was that we only had $4,000, and it was only three weeks away. Our people stepped up, and Jesus knocked it out of the park. People are hungry to show the love of God in a real way. We chose neighborhoods that fit our vision, where we have long-term holistic ministry work. These are places where we were already tutoring, had people living near, and team members who are present there. It was a huge, wide brush to paint with love. Pastor Brad Leach once said, "Good works lead to goodwill, which can lead to the Good News." We found that to be so true! We had an idea to clean a stranger's house. Well, it is a strange idea, but we thought it would be neat and felt it was from Jesus… so here we go. One of our leaders (Rhett) was sent with the task to knock on doors and see if

someone would let us clean. One amazing woman, Jenna, said, "Maybe I have to talk to my boyfriend first." The deadline was fast approaching for us to lock a house in, and we needed a confirmation. Rhett followed up, and she mentioned her boyfriend was quite skeptical, and he then asked if I would go, and maybe we could do some final persuasion. They ended up saying yes, especially when we told them, 'Hey, we know this is kind of weird, but we think Jesus wants us to do this for someone, and he picked you.' That house cleaning changed their lives forever. They laughed, and they came to City Life eventually. Not only did Jenna join our Dream Team, but just this past month, her boyfriend Jay got baptized and also joined the Dream Team as well.

We have a street in our town that many say is the worst in town. People say, "Don't go there or you will get shot." What people forget is where there are people, there are God's creations made in his image. So that is exactly where we went for our "Knock Knock" groceries night. We basically show up at someone's door and say, "Hey, we got some snacks and food for your Friday night, hope you enjoy!" We include a card that says, you are loved, belong, and have purpose. We then invited them back to our weekend celebration. The night was ending, and it was getting dark. One of our team members Lacey had one bag left and felt she needed go to one more house. This woman comes out and can't believe it. She goes on to say they are out of money, and that her assistance doesn't come for weeks, and was just wondering what they would do. It was a sign for her that Jesus loved her and was listening. You can see it now, the tears, the hugs... but it didn't stop there. She came to church, got baptized, and is now greeting families on Sundays at the main kids' doors as a Dream Team member. What! Come on, Jesus! God was orchestrating divine timing over and over again. I hope this inspires you to keep loving your city, typing this reminds me too. Let's dream big. The Good News is better than we can imagine, and a simple pack of gum and telling someone Jesus loves them can transform their life forever."

There are churches that I regularly pour into and consult. As we started doing Love Our City Week, there were several others who learned from us and started one in their city. We're excited to see this movement grow to more and more cities. Welcome to the Love Our City Movement!

LOVE LESSON:

There is nothing new under the sun. Take ideas and remix them for your own context.

LOVE QUESTION:

Have you ever been part of something great that you watched spread and grow into a movement?

LOVE APPLICATION:

How can you apply this devotional to your life?

LOVE NOTES:

What stuck out to you?

What else is God saying to you?

LOVE our City — WEEK 4 VIDEO SERIES

PLAY VIDEO

1. As Believers in Christ we are called to

_____ the atmosphere around us.

"Choose a good reputation over great riches; being held in high esteem is better than silver or gold." - Proverbs 22:1 NLT

2. We are called to be God's _____:

A person who acts as a representative or a promoter.

* 1 Corinthians 5:16-21

3. Is your APPEAL - _____?

4. The way to get closer to God, step into your calling and truly love your city starts with _____.

5. Betterment can do some good, but development is even better as it _____ people to become self-sustainable and build their own capacity.

6. Getting someone out of poverty or brokenness is not an _____, it's a _____.

DISCUSSION QUESTIONS

1. Have you ever seen the atmosphere shift when a solid Christian or several solid Christians came into the mix? (At your job, or school, or in a family situation)

* Read Proverbs 22:1

2. What is the reputation of Christians and Churches in your community?

* Read 1 Corinthians 5:16-21

3. What could reconciliation look like in your city?

4. How does your appeal for God look? How can it improve? (Get honest – it's the last session)

5. What does your regular prayer and devotional rhythm look like? How can it improve?

6. What are some ways you can give people a hand up in your city?

7. What is next for you, your group, and your church now that Love Our City is finishing for this season?

DAY 29

OUR JUSTICE

"Learn to do good; seek justice, correct oppression; bring justice to the fatherless, plead the widow's cause."
— Isaiah 1:17 ESV

"Check Nehemiah 5, he confronted injustice / Stood up for the forgotten / We need to discuss this / Because our planet has a leadership crisis / From Greece, to Russia, to China, to Isis"

"EMPOWERING OTHERS" - URBAN D. FEAT. D MAUB & YOUNG NOAH
(REBUILD ALBUM)

That word "Justice" can cause some Christians to hesitate. There have been some social justice movements that emphasized good works and excluded the gospel. Justice is not meant to be a replacement of the gospel - it should be a result of the gospel. The definition of justice is "just behavior or treatment. If you have a relationship with Jesus, then we should have just behavior and treatment towards our neighbors. Why? Because justice is part of God's character. Psalm 33:5 (NIV) says, "The Lord loves righteousness and justice; the earth is full of his unfailing love." In Psalm 146:7, the scriptures tell us, "He gives justice to the oppressed and food to the hungry. The Lord frees the prisoners." The calling of Jesus was prophesied about in the Old Testament. He was called to bring justice. Matthew 12:18 quotes this prophecy about the Messiah as it says, "Look at my Servant, whom I have chosen. He is my Beloved, who pleases me. I will put my Spirit upon him, and he will proclaim justice to the nations."

We are called to bring justice to our neighbors. Let me remind you that it doesn't only mean the neighbors that look like us, think like us, and vote like us. It also means to the ones who are different than us. It even means the ones who are oppressed, hungry, and in bondage. When Jesus shared the two greatest commandments, He was quoting scripture from the Old Testament. The first verse is from Deuteronomy 6:5, and the second is from Leviticus 19:9-18.

This passage in Leviticus goes into detail about how we should practice justice towards our neighbors around us in our city. Imagine if we did these things:

▷ **Live generously towards the poor and the foreigners. (vs.9-10)**

▷ **Don't steal. (vs. 11)**

▷ **Don't deceive or cheat anyone. (vs. 11)**

▷ **Don't defraud, rob or exploit people. (vs. 13)**

▷ **Don't disrespect deaf or blind people. (vs. 14)**

▷ **Don't twist justice by being partial to the poor or showing favor to the rich. Judge honestly. (vs. 15)**

▷ **Don't gossip. (vs. 16)**

▷ **Stand up for your neighbor when they are threatened. (vs. 16)**

▷ **Don't hate your brother or sister. (vs. 17)**

▷ **Don't seek revenge or hold a grudge, but love your neighbor as yourself. (vs. 18)**

Did you know that when we love our neighbors, it actually fulfills the law? Paul mentions this twice in Romans 13:8-10, where it says, "Owe nothing to anyone – except for your obligation to love one another.

If you love your neighbor, you will fulfill the requirements of God's law. For the commandments say, 'You must not commit adultery. You must not murder. You must not steal. You must not covet.' These – and other such commandments – are summed up in this one commandment: 'Love your neighbor as yourself.' Love does no wrong to others, so love fulfills the requirements of God's law." When Paul says owe nothing to anyone in context, he is talking about our debts. It doesn't mean that we should never borrow anything. It doesn't mean we shouldn't borrow any money, but it means that we pay our taxes, our mortgages, and our payments on time. We can pay those things down and pay them off. But our obligation to love one another is not something that we pay down or pay off.

As Christians, it is something we are obligated to continue to do. I know that the word obligation can have somewhat of a negative vibe to it. But Paul is teaching us that every debt that can be paid off should be paid off with love. Turn every behavior into an act of love. Love for God turns into a visible manifestation when we love others. That is what biblical justice is all about!

LOVE LESSON:

Justice is not meant to be a replacement of the gospel - it should be a result of the gospel.

LOVE QUESTION:

How can you better live out Isaiah 1:17 in your life?

LOVE APPLICATION:

How can you apply this devotional to your life?

LOVE NOTES:

What stuck out to you?

What else is God saying to you?

DAY 30

OUR DREAM

"I am in them, and you are in me. May they experience such perfect unity that the world will know that you sent me and that you love them as much as you love me."
— John 17:23 NLT

"Imagine a city where churches work together / There's no competition – just a kingdom endeavor / It gets no better / Imagine impact you could measure / That goes beyond attendance at a sermon or lecture"

"NEW LIFE, NEW FAM, NEW CITY" - URBAN D. (REBUILD ALBUM)

Our dream should reflect Jesus' vision for the church when he prayed in John 17 that believers would be in complete unity so the world would know the love of God. To an outsider, Christ followers can seem divided at times. There are some Christ followers that are extremely conservative, some that are more liberal, some that are inward focused, some that are outward focused, some that are out of touch, some that are culturally relevant, some that are engaged in social justice, and some that are engaged in politics. We could go on and on listing the different styles, methods, passions, and theological leanings that Christians and churches have. All those differences are not always a bad thing, but dream with me for a minute... what if the capital C church was known for truly loving their cities? What if we were known for following the words of Jesus, where we authentically loved our neighbors as ourselves? That is one thing we could rally around!

Unfortunately, in many communities, the church can be viewed as a parasite. It comes in and sucks out resources. But what if the reputation of the church was different everywhere? What if it were positive? What if we were known for being a place that poured out resources? It could be known as a place to find healing, hope, friendships, and answers. Imagine if Christians were known for bringing people together, empowering them, and making their communities a better place. Even people who don't agree with our message would still respect and appreciate the work that we do in our cities. The church should be a life source that radically makes its community better, both spiritually and physically. Imagine if the city looked to the church for solutions when crisis and tragedy hit. I regularly challenge church leaders with the following questions: If your church closed its doors today, would your neighborhood even notice? Would they care? Would it impact them?

The church is in need of a rebrand. Loving our cities can change the narrative! We are seeing our dream slowly but surely come to fruition in our city. As we continue to love our community, the reputation of churches is growing more and more positive. Several pastors and Christian leaders are sitting in community leadership positions to help leverage change in policies and major redevelopment decisions happening in our districts. The events and programs our churches put on are partnering with government and businesses to meet tangible needs, including backpacks, school supplies, Christmas gifts, food, job training, job fairs, rehab programs, mentoring, and more. The church is being invited to these positions because of the positive influence we have developed. It is also happening in several other cities around the world.

Our dream is that churches everywhere would get more involved in loving their city as they follow the instructions of Jesus. It goes way beyond community service projects.. Our dream is that this is a primer to get you set up to turn this into your new normal. We pray you will begin to look through new frames at your everyday life and see opportunities all around you. Our dream is that this would become a multiplication movement that would go viral around the world. We believe this could be the beginning of the next great awakening of the church as we learn to love our city and point people to Jesus.

LOVE LESSON:

The church can be and should be a life source that radically makes the community better, both physically and spiritually.

LOVE QUESTION:

If your church closed tomorrow, would your community notice? How would it impact them?

LOVE APPLICATION:

How can you apply this devotional to your life?

LOVE NOTES:

What stuck out to you?

What else is God saying to you?

30

LOVE
our City

LOVE our City — WEEK 5 VIDEO SERIES

PLAY VIDEO 5

▷ **1.** "Also, seek the peace and prosperity of the city to which I have carried you into exile. Pray to the Lord for it, because if it prospers, you too will prosper." - Jeremiah 29:7 NLT

2. I want my city to _____, so I can prosper!

3. I can't do EVERYTHING, but I must do _____!

4. Loving our city is about FAITHFUL _____ - Showing up, listening, serving, and reflecting Jesus in ordinary places.

5. The question is not what we did, but who we are _____.

BONUS SESSION

DISCUSSION QUESTIONS

1. Have you ever experienced a major transition like moving to a new city, school, job, or season of life?

2. What made that transition difficult or uncomfortable?

Key Thought - God often places us in environments that stretch us - Not to isolate us, but to shape us.

3. What problems in our city feel overwhelming?

4. How does shifting from trying to do "Everything" to "Something" change our mindset?

5. What is a possible "Something" for you to start doing?

6. How is Faithful Presence different from one-time events, or short term service? What could that look like in your life and your city?

7. Over the past 30 days, how has God began to change your heart? What could it look like to continue this journey beyond the book?

Closing Action Steps:
› Pray for your city.
› Pray for Clarity and courage to act with your next steps.
› Pray for others in your group and their "Something".

SOURCES

DAY 2:

[1] World Bank Group "Poverty, Prosperity, and Planet Report 2024" worldbank.org

[2] Melissa Kollar and Zach Scherer, "Income in the United States: 2024" census.gov September 9, 2025.

DAY 5:

[1] Caleb Mathis, "5 Revival Movements to get us ready for the next one" crossroads.net

[2] "New Research: Belief in Jesus Rises, Fueled by Younger Adults" barna.com April 7, 2025.

[3] "New Barn Data: Young Adults Lead a Resurgence in Church Attendance" barna.com Sept. 2, 2025.

[4] Maria Sherman, "How Christian artists are winning over listeners and entering pop's mainstream" apnews.com December 24, 2025.

[5] Ed Boice, "Forrest Frank Surpasses Drake in YouTube Music Listeners" rapzilla.com August 18, 2025.

[6] Bob Smietana, "Bible sales keep growing, even as many Americans lose their religion" apnews.com November 24, 2025.

DAY 6:

[1] Carissa Wong, "Four-fifths of the world's population now live in urban areas" newscientist.com November 18, 2025.

[2] Bret Boyd, "Urbanization and the mass movement of people to cities." graylinegroup.com

[3] William H. Frey "2020 Census: Big cities grew and became more diverse, especially among their youth" **brookings.edu** October 28, 2021.

[4] Valarie Strauss, "For the first time, minority students expected to be majority in U.S. public schools this fall" **washingtonpost.com** Aug. 21, 2014.

[5] "Racial/Ethnic Enrollment in Public Schools" **www.nces.ed.gov** May 2024.

[6] Faith Communities Today "Fact 2020 Survey Results" **faithcommunitiestoday.org**

DAY 12:

[1] Andrew Chow, "ChatGPT may be eroding critical thinking skills, according to a new MIT study" **time.com** June 23, 2025.

DAY 13:

[1] Clark Mendock, "Americans throw away 150,000 tons of food everyday" **independent.co.uk** April 4, 2018.

[2] "Consumption by the United States" **public.wsu.edu**

DAY 18:

[1] Bill Easum, "10 church stats you need to know for 2018" **www.reachrightstudios.com**

[2] Mark Deymaz, "Outeach Magazine – Ethnic Blends" **outreachmagazine .com/Deymaz**

[3] Sam Eaton, "59% of millennials raised in church have dropped out – and they're trying to tell us why" **faithit.com** April 4, 2018.

DAY 19:

[1] Richard Alleyne, "Welcome to the information age – 174 newspapers a day" **telegraph.co.uk** Feb. 11, 2011.

[2] ibid.

ABOUT THE AUTHOR

TOMMY URBAN D. KYLLONEN

Tommy "Urban D." Kyllonen has been in ministry for over 30 years at Crossover Church in Tampa, Florida. He has been the lead pastor for over 24 years. Under his leadership the church has seen 30x growth.

his multi-ethnic, multi-generational, multi-class church has become a model. As they grew, they relocated into a 43,000-square foot retail building that was a former Toys R' Us in Tampa's Uptown District. Outreach Magazine recognized Crossover as one of America's Most Innovative Churches. Crossover has also been featured in USA Today, Newsweek, CBS News, BET News, and several regional media outlets. Urban D. is an internationally known hip-hop artist who has released nine full-length albums and several remix projects (www.urband.org).

Tommy has authored seven books. His most acclaimed book "Love Our City" is a devotional format for churches and small groups to go through together. The video series was available on Right Now Media. It also includes a community service project aspect. His church has used this to reach thousands of new people. They created a leaders box kit that gives churches all the tools to launch Love Our City. There are hundreds of churches that have joined the Love Our City Movement. Tommy has a passion to help other leaders win. He founded the Flavor Fest Urban Leadership Conference, which has trained over 7,000 leaders (www.flavorfest.org). Tommy has coached over a hundred pastors and currently leads The Urban Church Network with dozens of churches involved (www.urbanchurchnetwork.com). He lives in Tampa, Florida with his wife Lucy and his two daughters Deyana and Sophia.

www.ingramcontent.com/pod-product-compliance
Lightning Source LLC
Chambersburg PA
CBHW071142130626
46553CB00004B/1489